SWEATING IT OUT

What the "Experts" Say Causes Poverty

Michael L. Landon

University Press of America,® Inc.
Lanham · Boulder · New York · Toronto · Oxford

Copyright © 2006 by
Michael L. Landon

University Press of America,® Inc.
4501 Forbes Boulevard
Suite 200
Lanham, Maryland 20706
UPA Acquisitions Department (301) 459-3366

PO Box 317
Oxford
OX2 9RU, UK

Library of Congress Control Number: 2006924821
ISBN-13: 978-0-7618-3520-2 (clothbound : alk. paper)
ISBN-10: 0-7618-3520-2 (clothbound : alk. paper)
ISBN-13: 978-0-7618-3521-9 (paperback : alk. paper)
ISBN-10: 0-7618-3521-0 (paperback : alk. paper)

DEDICATION

I dedicate this book to my wife, Susan, and our three children, Angela, Cynthia, and Michael, who wholeheartedly and joyfully lived with the consequences of my decisions to be a missionary, student, minister and teacher.

CONTENTS

Introduction   1

Section I - What the Experts Say Causes Poverty   9
Chapter 1 – The Culture of Poverty   11
Chapter 2 – Economic Ethos   21
Chapter 3 – Personal Irresponsibility   29
Chapter 4 – Dependency Theory   33
Chapter 5 – U.S. Adaptations of Culture of Poverty   39
Chapter 6 – U.S. Structural Problems   47
Chapter 7 – Stress Model   53
Chapter 8 – Summary of Experts' Explanations   59

Section II – What Low Income Adults Say Causes Poverty   63
Chapter 9 – The Context of Hammond, LA   65
Chapter 10 – Bob and Carla's Story   69
Chapter 11 – Don's Story   81
Chapter 12 – Evelyn's Story   89
Chapter 13 – Mary's Story   99
Chapter 14 – Olivia's Story   107
Chapter 15 – Conclusions about Informants' Explanations
                for Poverty   119

Section III – Biblical & Theological Reflections on Poverty   123
Chapter 16 – Biblical Definitions and Presuppositions
                about Poverty   125
Chapter 17 – The Old Testament on Poverty   129
Chapter 18 – The New Testament on Poverty   139
Chapter 19 – Christian Reflections on Poverty   143

Section IV – Implications & Suggestions for Action   157
Chapter 20 – Implications for Christians   159
Chapter 21 – Suggestions for Christian Action   167

Author's Biographical Sketch   187
Index   189

LIST OF FIGURES

0.1	Preliminary Grid of Explanations for Poverty	5
2.1	Harrison's What Makes Development Happen	22
8.1	Fitting the Experts' Explanations Together	60
20.1	Chewning's Biblically Authenticated Business, Economics, and Public Policy	166

LIST OF TABLES

1.1	Culture of Poverty Pattern	14
2.1	Economic Ethos Pattern	25
3.1	Personal Irresponsibility Pattern	31
4.1	Dependency Theory Pattern	35
5.1	Human Resources Pattern	41
5.2	Welfare Culture Pattern	43
5.3	Material Resources Pattern	44
5.4	Underclass Pattern	46
6.1	U. S. Structural Problems Pattern	49
7.1	Stress Model Pattern	57
10.1	Causes of Poverty in General According to Bob	75
10.2	Causes of Bob's Own Low Income	76
10.3	Causes of Poverty in General According to Carla	78
10.4	Causes of Carla's Own Low Income	79
11.1	Causes of Poverty in General According to Don	85
11.2	Causes of Don's Own Low Income	86
12.1	Causes of Poverty in General According to Evelyn	95
12.2	Causes of Evelyn's Own Low Income	98
13.1	Causes of Poverty in General According to Mary	104
13.2	Causes of Mary's Own Low Income	105
14.1	Causes of Poverty in General According to Olivia	113
14.2	Causes of Olivia's Own Low Income	115
15.1	Average of Grids of Explanations for Poverty in General According to Race and Income Source (Welfare or Working)	120
15.2	Average of Grids of Explanations for Own Low Income According to Race and Income Source (Welfare or Working)	121

INTRODUCTION

During a very difficult year in my life, I finally took personally what I had seen and learned about poverty while a missionary in Brazil. There I saw people who worked very hard just barely surviving as they fought through the daily battles of hours on crowded buses, malnourished children, overpriced and crowded housing and schools that filled up and closed their doors to their children. I remembered this horrible account written by a Catholic priest.

> One day, in the arid region of northeastern Brazil, one of the most famine-stricken parts of the world, I met a bishop going into his house; he was shaking. "Bishop, what's the matter?" I asked. He replied that he had just seen a terrible sight: in front of the cathedral was a woman with three small children and a baby clinging to her neck. He saw that they were fainting from hunger. The baby seemed to be dead. He said: "Give the baby some milk, woman!" "I can't, sir," she answered. The bishop went on insisting that she should, and she that she could not. Finally, because of his insistence, she opened her blouse. Her breast was bleeding; the baby sucked violently at it. And sucked blood.[1]

Millions of people through out the world are poor, and many are desperately poor, like this woman. Although so many situations like this seem so far away from North Americans cloistered away in comfortable homes, they are real, and similar situations, perhaps not quite as bad, are nearby. During the last few years, the debate on welfare has brought poverty to everyone's attention, but the debate seems to have

---

[1] Leonardo Boff and Clodovis Boff, *Introducing Liberation Theology,* trans. Paul Burns (Maryknoll, N.Y.: Orbis Books, 1987), 1-2.

concentrated on rhetoric about middle class taxes, not on understanding poverty.

But if it's not about your pocketbook, why should you care? Why should you take time out of a busy life to read about poverty?

Motivations for Understanding Poverty

There are at least four major reasons why this is important to all of us, but the first two are the disastrous consequences of ignorance.

Looking for Solutions

The ignorance of the causes and effects of poverty has not only led to ineffective programs, but sometimes has led to barbaric demands, such as the bishop demanded in the situation related above.

Understanding Others

The second problem is that the poor have been looked down upon and slandered just for being poor, even "demonized" by many.[2]

> I don't understand why they should hate me so much, just for getting welfare. I'm just trying to take care of my child as best as I know how right now. Sure, I made mistakes, but I didn't break any laws. And now I am trying to get myself together and give me and my daughter a future. Welfare is not so much that it is going to break down the government to help us. And if I don't do it, foster care or orphanages cost more and will hurt her more. So why don't they just give us this little bit of nothing and stop acting like we are criminals or something?[3]

I'm not sure that being middle class or higher implies good character. Nor do I think that all poor people or those on welfare are evil. Sound-bite journalism has reduced financial well-being to short, simplistic, and often moralistic clichés, while real life is messy and harder to deal with.

Democracy

A third reason to study poverty is the principle of liberty for all. When experts regularly take it upon themselves to speak for people,

---

[2] Ruth Sidel, "The Enemy Within: A Commentary on the Demonization of Difference," *American Journal of Orthopsychiatry* 66 (1996): 490.

[3] Johnson in Ann Withorn, "'Why Do They Hate Me So Much?' A History of Welfare and Its Abandonment in the United States," *American Journal of Orthopsychiatry* 66 (1996): 496.

often to the point of excluding them from the discussion, they will soon be seen as incapable, and then as objects to be manipulated until proper results are achieved. Many poor people have been treated this way since the "War on Poverty" of the 1960's.

This was demonstrated in the 1990's in a discussion in which the author participated with the leaders of community service organizations. When asked, "What does our needy community need?" they asked for a number of financial investments to help their organizations function more easily. When the author commented that the group was discussing their institutional needs rather than the poor community's needs, one leader responded, "Well, we're the ones present. That's what we need to talk about." Somehow, when only the "experts" are at the table, the results seem to be one-sided.

One of the main purposes of this book is to present both what the experts say causes poverty and what low income people say about the causes. According to Slim and Thompson, oral testimony from the poor a) allows the poor to define themselves rather than be defined by others, b) makes the development establishment accountable to the poor also, c) emphasizes the diversity of the human experience and serves as a challenge to generalizations and simplistic, mechanistic views of poverty, d) expresses their own values and presents their own techniques for coping with difficulties, e) draws out interdisciplinary approaches to research and development.[4]

Christian Concern

A fourth reason to study poverty is important for those who call themselves Christians. While it is true that Jesus said, "The poor you will always have with you" (Matthew 26:11)[5], he was not brushing them aside. He began his ministry by declaring

> The Spirit of the Lord is on me,
> because he has anointed me
> to preach good news to the poor.
> He has sent me to proclaim freedom for the prisoners
> and recovery of sight for the blind,
> to release the oppressed,
> to proclaim the year of the Lord's favor. (Luke 4:18-19)

---

[4] Hugo Slim and Paul Thompson, *Listening for a Change* (Philadelphia: New Society Publishers, 1995), 2-8.

[5] All quotations from the Bible will be from the New International Version.

Jesus also made it plain that every Christian's dealing with the needy is central his own relationship with God in Matthew 25.

> Then he will say to those on his left, "Depart from me, you who are cursed, into the eternal fire prepared for the devil and his angels. For I was hungry and you gave me nothing to eat, I was thirsty and you gave me nothing to drink, I was a stranger and you did not invite me in, I needed clothes and you did not clothe me, I was sick and in prison and you did not look after me." (Matthew 25:41-43)

For some reason that we may not understand, Jesus identified with the poor, hurting and outcast. And it is very simple—if his disciples turn their back on the poor, they turn their back on Jesus. Thus, one cannot simply assign only leftover importance, energy and money to benevolence! To be Jesus' disciple means to imitate him.

Yet, why should you trust me? Why should you read this book on poverty?

Where Did I Get the Information?

How was the research presented in this book done? Who were the sources of information, and how was the information handled?

An Applied Christian Commitment

When I first began to think seriously about poverty, I was already a missionary in Brazil. From the beginning, I had a commitment to understand poverty from God's point of view. Based on my cross-cultural experiences I already had in Brazil, I knew that I couldn't just assume what I used to—that poor people are poor because they're lazy. I began to read the Bible in light of some specific Christians that I now knew who were good and hard working, but very poor.

Poverty According to the Experts

I also began to take classes at a seminary in Brazil that was strongly committed to South American Liberation Theology. In response to the violent attack on Capitalism by students and faculty, I started reading everything I could get my hands on in the areas of economy and political theory to verify and balance their perspectives. From both the religious and secular material, I perceived four explanations for poverty by the experts. They were labeled by using their own key words: (1) Culture of Poverty, (2) Economic Ethos, (3) Personal Irresponsibility and (4) Structural Sin.

As the following chapters will explain, these explanations for poverty can be placed on a grid that demonstrates how they emphasize different explanations for the cause of poverty, as seen in Figure 0.1. The two axes represent differing answers to two fundamental questions: (1) is the cause of poverty primarily a way of thinking or a way of acting, and (2) is the cause of poverty located in the poor themselves, or in the society as a whole?

Figure 0.1
Preliminary Grid of Explanations for Poverty

	Personal Cause	Structural Cause
Reason lies:		
Inside (ways of thinking)	Culture of Poverty	Economic Ethos
Outside (behavior, social structures, etc.)	Personal Irresponsibility	Structural Sin

As time went on, and I had the opportunity to study in the U.S., an additional six explanations for poverty were discovered in sociological and anthropological literature and fit into the same grid of the two axes. All ten of these will be presented and explained in the next section of chapters.

Poverty According to Low Income Adults

A specific goal of this research was to compare these rival theories of poverty with the explanations of low-income adults in the Hammond, Louisiana area. Four groups of low-income adults were sampled to encourage variety and allow some comparisons based on economic status and ethnicity. The first two groups were the Caucasian and African American population of government dependent adults—those that depend on "welfare." The maximum income limits for this group ranged from an annual income of $8550 to $16,100, depending on how many dependents are in the household. The second two groups were the Caucasian and African American working poor—these earned less than $13,650 to $25,750 per year, depending on the number of dependents. These may have qualified for "welfare," but did not receive it at the time of the interview. They did often receive reduced school lunches, help in housing and earned income benefits.

No Hispanic or other minorities were interviewed since the census and practical experience indicated that they made up no more than 1% of the local population, which is very small compared to the African American and Caucasian low income families which made up about 40% of the population.

At least two adults were interviewed from each of the four populations. They were selected according to standard anthropological procedures from the varied contacts the author had in the community.

But, can such a small number of interviewees really tell us anything about poverty? Yes, they can, within certain limitations.

What This Research Can Tell Us

Comments from these low-income adults can support current theories or explanations about poverty by the experts, but they cannot prove or disprove the causes of poverty. One reason is because their perspectives may be clouded by presuppositions, defensiveness, etc. Another is the scientific principle that generally only repeated, controlled experiments can prove causality.

This kind of research and writing does have several important strengths:

1. It has collected and compared explanations for poverty from many different sources into a convenient single source. This facilitates an introduction to the study of poverty and comparison of the theories.

2. It has recorded the perspectives of low-income adults about poverty that show life through their eyes. This gives several different perspectives and explanations, but more importantly, it gives detail and life to a subject that is often left to numbers and percentages only. Besides providing information on the causes of poverty, this research describes the neighborhood and housing of the informants, and lets them tell their own life story—how they got in this situation.

3. This kind of information also helps inform those who want to assist low-income families to understand what the poor think is significant and where to begin working together.

4. These comments can provide new theories to be considered and evaluated by the experts.

5. This writing takes very seriously God's perspective on poverty as revealed in the Bible and the Christian commitment to follow his instructions in this matter.

Outline

This book begins with a section of several chapters presenting the ten theories of poverty from the experts. These theories have likely influenced most of the readers, so this section will help the reader sort out his own set of presuppositions as he begins this study. The second section presents the life stories, living conditions and explanations for poverty from six low-income adults. The third section contains several chapters of Biblical and theological reflections on poverty. While the author considers this Biblical material to be fundamental and author-itative, the first two sections precede it since they may open the reader's eyes to new possibilities. The fourth and last section does some analysis of the previous material and gives some suggestions for those who want to make a difference.

SECTION I
WHAT THE EXPERTS SAY CAUSES POVERTY

I found ten different explanations for poverty formulated by the experts. Four explanations that tend to operate in the international discussion of poverty are presented in the first four chapters. They are then compared and analyzed in a chapter, and then the remaining six explanations that arise from North American social research are presented. A concluding chapter will fit all ten of the explanations for poverty on the same grid.

The four international explanations:
Culture of Poverty
Economic Ethos
Personal Irresponsibility
Dependency Theory

The six North American explanations:
Human Resources
Material Resources
Welfare Culture
Underclass
Stress
U. S. Structural Problems

CHAPTER 1
THE CULTURE OF POVERTY

This term is associated with Oscar Lewis, a well known anthropologist, and was first used by him in his book, *Five Families* (1959). He gave his fullest explanation in the book called *The Children of Sanchez* (1961), and then basically repeated that information in several later publications. The basic thesis of the Culture of Poverty explanation is that some people are poor because their culture or way of life is faulty. This culture, "or, more accurately, as a subculture with its own structure and rationale, as a way of life . . . is passed down from generation to generation along family lines."[1]

The concept, however, is much older than Lewis' use. This section on this explanation for poverty includes a presentation of the early proponents of the concept, the role of authors such as Myrdal, Lewis, Moynihan and Harrison in popularizing the theory, and finally, the criticism of the Culture of Poverty explanation.

Early Versions of the Culture of Poverty
The first traces of the culture of poverty explanation began with the founding of the American Economic Association by Richard Ely and Amasa Walker, who believed that both the African American and the "southern and eastern European immigrants were genetically inferior."[2] Evidently, the intent was not malevolent since two of these

---

[1] Oscar Lewis, *A Study of Slum Culture* (New York: Random House, 1968), 4.
[2] Robert Cherry, "The Culture-of-Poverty Thesis and African-Americans: The Work of Gunnar Myrdal and Other Institutionalists," *Journal of Economic Issues* 29, no. 4 (December 1995): 1119.

"progressive economists," Richard Ely and John R. Commons, were prominent leaders in the Social Gospel Movement of the late 1800's, which proposed a "Christianized, non-Marxist socialism."[3] Commons thought that African Americans were so present-oriented and genetically inferior that they could never compete with Americans of European descent and "only cross-breeding would allow African Americans to rise up to the standards of European Americans".[4]

Although Booker T. Washington rejected the genetic inequality of the African American, he did "believe that African Americans were culturally inferior to whites."[5] He pointed to the substantial progress of the enslaved blacks over the African blacks as proof that the race could advance.[6] He also maintained that this cultural problem that tended to produce poverty was often accentuated by the social problem of moving from a rural environment to an urban setting.[7]

Myrdal Creates a Stereotype

Myrdal's classic work on poverty, *An American Dilemma*, is an enormous, multi-volume work that is hard to locate, much less read. Thankfully, numerous reviews have been written, and some important implications can be noted.

Myrdal was a Swedish economist, whose primary purpose seemed to be to increase white Americans' guilt over racism.[8] Myrdal seemed to have been walking a tightrope between criticizing the black culture without blaming the people. Herskovits' recently published *Myth of the Negro Past*,[9] which pointed out the remnants of African cultures in current African American culture and seemed to point the finger at African Americans for their own poverty, was a particular pain to Myrdal.

---

[3] R. A. Gonce, "The Social Gospel, Ely, and Commons's Initial Stage of Thought," *Journal of Economic Issues* 30, no. 3 (September 1996): 641-44.

[4] Cherry, "Culture-of-Poverty," 1120-21.

[5] Ibid., 1122.

[6] Booker T. Washington, *The Negro in the South*, reprint ed. (New York: Carol Publishing, 1907), 59-60.

[7] Cherry, "Culture-of-Poverty," 1123.

[8] David W. Southern, *Gunner Myrdal and Black-White Relations: The Use and Abuse of An American Dilemma* (Baton Rouge: Louisiana State University Press, 1987), 44, 55; Cherry, "Culture-of-Poverty," 1127-28.

[9] Melville J. Herskovits, *The Myth of the Negro Past* (New York: Harper, 1941).

Myrdal thought that he could solve the problem by declaring that the black culture was a "distorted development or a pathological condition."[10] In other words,

> the Negro problem was really a white problem. . . . He stressed that the Negro's entire life was in some way or another a reaction to white pressure.[11]

Yet, what stuck in people's minds was the negative stereotype. According to Cherry, "every example of the negative stereotypes identified by [President] Johnson [in his War on Poverty] shows up in *An American Dilemma* as attributes of lower-class African Americans."[12]

Commons and Myrdal were both considered institutional economists, "who emphasized the crucial role of institutions and structural factors" in determining social conditions.[13] Why then did they embrace the Culture of Poverty explanation that stressed cultural factors? "For both economists, culture-of-poverty theories were useful in arguing against those who claimed that more radical anti-capitalist institutional changes were necessary," a tactic which probably continues even today![14] Thus, in his attempt to defend American capitalism, Myrdal ended up perpetuating a stereotype of African Americans that he abhorred!

Lewis Develops and Popularizes a Theory

While Myrdal and others' work went along with the popular negative stereotypes of African Americans, Lewis studied Latin Americans and described the Culture of Poverty as being composed of some seventy traits that transcended even national and cultural boundaries, being found in a portion of the poor in many parts of the world. These traits can be categorized into five areas: (1) family structure, (2) interpersonal relationships, (3) time orientation, (4) value systems and (5) spending patterns.[15] See complete list in Table 1.1.

---

[10] Southern, *Gunner Myrdal*, 45.
[11] Ibid., 56.
[12] Cherry, "Culture-of-Poverty," 1127.
[13] Ibid., 1128.
[14] Ibid.
[15] Lewis, *Slum Culture*, 4.

Table 1.1
Culture of Poverty Pattern

1. Family Structure
     a. no childhood
     b. early sex
     c. many abandoned wives and children*
     d. consensual marriages*
     e. mother-centered families
     f. know maternal relatives better
     g. authoritarianism, machismo / martyr complex among
        women
     h. lack of privacy
     i. verbal family solidarity / real sibling rivalry

2. Interpersonal Relationships
     a. feelings of marginality, helplessness, dependence,
        inferiority
     b. maternal deprivation
     c. orality
     d. weak ego structure
     e. confused sexual ID
     f. lack of impulse control (impulsive)
     g. male superiority
     h. high tolerance for psychological pathologies
     i. violence common
     j. alcoholism common

3. Time Orientation
     a. present orientation
     b. little deferred gratification and plans for future
     c. fatalism

4. Value Systems
     a. aware of middle class values, but don't live them
     b. provincial, little sense of history*
     c. low education, literacy*
     d. not participate in labor unions, political parties,
        medical care, national security retirement, banks,
        art galleries, department stores*

    e. distrust of police, government, institutions
    f. easily manipulated by protest movements

5. Spending Patterns
    a. don't own property
    b. unemployment, underemployment
    c. low wages, unskilled jobs
    d. no savings
    e. chronic shortage of cash
    f. little food reserves, frequent buying small amounts
    g. pawning of personal goods
    h. informal credit among friends and relatives
    i. borrowing from local moneylenders at high interest
    j. second hand furniture and clothing
    k. rent, not own home

6. Community level
    a. poor housing, overcrowding
    b. gregariousness
    c. esprit de corps
    d. territoriality
    e. minimum of social org. above family*

Sources: drawn from Lewis 1961(1963): xxvi-xxxvii; 1965: xlvi-
xlvii; 1968:4,7-11; Leeds 1971, 239-41.

Lewis admitted that this Culture of Poverty was both a result of
and an adaptation to poverty, but he emphasized the perpetuating role
of the family in passing on this faulty culture.[16] To Wilson, Lewis was
saying that "these traits assume a 'life of their own'" and placed strong
emphasis on their autonomous nature beyond the control of individuals.[17] At one point, Lewis claimed, "by the time slum children are
age six or seven, they have usually absorbed the basic values and
attitudes of their subculture and are not psychologically geared to take
full advantage of changing conditions or increased opportunities which

---

[16] Ibid., 5-6.
[17] William J. Wilson, *The Truly Disadvantaged* (Chicago: University of Chicago Press: 1987), 137.

may occur in their lifetime."[18] Because of the popularity of his books, including several movie productions, Lewis was largely responsible for popularizing the Culture of Poverty explanation for poverty.

A Theory Adopted by A Government

Lewis' theory was brought to the nation's attention in another form through the famous Moynihan Report of 1965, entitled The Negro Family: The Case for National Action. This short report, which was admittedly incomplete and intended to be secret, appeared to recommend "white moral engineering of all black families instead of government programs for employment, job training and education. The white sociologist was in black parlance, 'blaming the victim.'"[19]

When Moynihan's message was re-communicated in President Johnson's speech "To Fulfill These Rights" on June 4, 1965 at Howard University, it was heartily accepted by blacks and used by many in educational and governmental areas.[20] Indeed, Johnson's "War on Poverty" of the 1960s seemed built on the Culture of Poverty theory, including his presumptive pledge to "untangle the 'pathology' of their [the Negro] family life," to use the words of Gettleman and Mermelstein.[21] Lewis didn't make these kinds of assertions, but by now, only parts of his work were being referenced.[22]

The Culture of Poverty explanation for poverty was adopted not just by the government, but also by a legion of researchers and social workers. To many, Harrington is even better known than Lewis because of his hearty endorsement of the phrases and concepts of the Culture of Poverty. The concepts being that "even when the money finally trickles down, even when a school is built in a poor neighborhood, for instance, the poor are still deprived. The entire environment, their life, their values, do not prepare them to take advantage of the new opportunity."[23]

---

[18] Oscar Lewis, "The Culture of Poverty," in On Understanding Poverty, ed. Daniel P. Moynihan (New York: Basic Books, 1968), 188.

[19] Southern, Gunner Myrdal, 267.

[20] Ibid.

[21] Marvin E. Gettleman and David Mermelstein, The Great Society Reader (New York: Vintage Books, 1967), 253.

[22] Wilson, Truly Disadvantaged, 13.

[23] Michael Harrington, The Other America: Poverty in the United States, revised ed. (Baltimore: Penguin Books, 1971), 10.

According to Harrington, "the poor are caught in a vicious circle."[24] He is aware of the holism of a culture and cites the "family structure," "language of the poor, a psychology of the poor, a world view of the poor," being "an internal alien," "a sense of hopelessness," "personal chaos" as elements of this culture of poverty.[25]

In short, being poor is not one aspect of a person's life in this country; it is his life. Taken as a whole, poverty is a culture. Taken on the family level, it has the same quality. These are people who lack education and skill, who have bad health, poor housing, low levels of aspiration and high level of mental distress. They are, in the language of sociology, "multi-problem families."[26]

While Lewis saw the Culture of Poverty within a small portion of the poor,[27] Harrington generalized it to the whole class, the "40,000,000 to 50,000,000 human beings" who lived in the invisible, other America.[28]

Criticisms of the Culture of Poverty Explanation

Despite governmental acceptance and support, the Culture of Poverty explanation has been roundly criticized. Early criticisms were published in books edited by Leacock and Valentine.[29] In the book by Leacock, Leeds and Valentine criticized Lewis' scientific analysis.

Valentine condensed the culture of poverty into five propositions: (1) lack of participation in the larger society by the poor, (2) different values, (3) no local social organization among the poor beyond the family, unstable family life and weak identity, (4) character and (5) worldview development.[30] Valentine then claimed that two are not true

---

[24] Ibid., 16.

[25] Ibid., 17-18, 170-71.

[26] Ibid., 171.

[27] Oscar Lewis, *La Vida: A Puerto Rican Family in the Culture of Poverty—San Juan and New York* (New York: Random House, 1965-1966), xlviii-xlix.

[28] Harrington, *Other America*, 19.

[29] Eleanor B. Leacock, *The Culture of Poverty: A Critique* (New York: Simon and Schuster, 1971); Charles A. Valentine, *Culture and Poverty* (Chicago: University of Chicago Press, 1968).

[30] Charles A. Valentine, "The Culture of Poverty: Its Scientific Significance and its Implications for Action," in *The Culture of Poverty: A Critique*, ed. Eleanor B. Leacock (New York: Simon and Schuster: 1971), 204-11.

to Lewis' own data and that the other three are much more the result of poverty than the cause of poverty.[31]

Miller also saw the poor as having pathological tendencies, but presented them as focal concerns of the poor (trouble, toughness, smartness, excitement, fate and autonomy), not culture of the poor.[32] Gans, as well, avoided speaking of "culture," using "class" instead. He suggested that the biggest difference was the female-based / marginalized male family structure.[33] Gans also postulated that the aspirations of the poor were not faulty, but realistic for their current socio-economic position.[34]

H. Lewis asked, "Culture of Poverty? What does it matter?" and responded, "It matters because it has become more ideological than scientific."[35] What was particularly evil about the Culture of Poverty explanation in the eyes of its critics was that it was taken as permission for the government and others to manipulate the poor family's way of life. Receipt of benefits was conditioned on proper behavior.

> Unemployment may make you feel sad and despairing, social security survivor's benefits may confuse you, but you will not be faced—as are women on welfare—with questions about your sex life, with being fingerprinted to prevent fraud, and with the need, now, to make new plans because your benefits will soon be transitional, even though your needs are not; nor, if you turn on the radio, are you likely to hear yourself insulted or discover yet another policy proposal that will profoundly undercut your efforts to help your family.[36]

---

[31] Ibid.

[32] Walter Miller, "Focal Concerns of Lower-Class Culture," in *Poverty in America*, new, expanded ed., edited by Louis A. Fernan, Joyce L. Kormmuh, and Alan Haber (Ann Arbor: Michigan State University Press, 1968), 397.

[33] Herbert J. Gans, "Subcultures and Class," in *Poverty in America*, new, expanded ed., edited by Louis A. Fernan, Joyce L. Kormmuh, and Alan Haber (Ann Arbor: Michigan State University Press, 1968), 446-47.

[34] Ibid., 450-52.

[35] Hylan Lewis, "Culture of poverty? What does it matter?" in *The Culture of Poverty: A Critique*, ed. Eleanor B. Leacock (New York: Simon and Schuster, 1971), 345.

[36] Ann Withorn, "'Why do they hate me so much?' A History of Welfare and its Abandonment in the United States," *American Journal of Orthopsychiatry* 66, no. 4 (October 1996): 496.

In the 1930s and 1940s some refused aid to black women to keep them working as field and domestic help. In the 1950s and 1960s they denied aid to many single mothers and women of color, using "unsuitable home," "man in the house," and "midnight raid" policies that equated unwed with unfit motherhood. The almost explicit goal was to make "the Welfare" a program hated by recipients and observers alike, rather than a springboard for better policies.[37]

Conclusion

Despite these criticisms, the Culture of Poverty explanation for poverty has been widely accepted and is a powerful force in government intervention in poverty even today. While Valentine charges that Lewis' empirical data does not support his conclusions, this material is not available to the author. Some of the criticism centers on Lewis' use of "culture" rather than "subculture," but this is relatively inconsequential.

Some of the criticisms of Lewis' work are likely correct, and many of the criticisms of the War on Poverty are correct, but at least some of Lewis' conclusions about some poor people seem evident to even the casual observer of poverty.

The main problem seems to be that people took Lewis' research to mean all poor people are culturally inferior and to justify manipulating the poor—things Lewis would never have done. Lewis had a respect for the poor that the War on Poverty never had.

---

[37] Ibid., 499.

CHAPTER 2
ECONOMIC ETHOS

The second explanation of the causes of poverty refers to a society's ethos in relation to the economy and has been developed by political theorists. Ethos is that general understanding of what is true and good in a society. It differs from the Culture of Poverty in that ethos refers to the society's way of thinking while the Culture of Poverty describes the way of the thinking of a subset of society, the poor. It differs from Dependency Theory that is explained later in that the Economic Ethos explanation assumes that ethos determines the social structures, while Dependency Theory assumes that the mode of production determines the ethos.

This explanation is often promoted by two groups who seemingly argue from different directions. One group is made up of economists and political theorists who argue and plan economic wealth for nations. Their key word is modernization. The other group is made up of North American Christians who plead for a return to the past. The main critics of this explanation are those who propose Dependency Theory, the economic basis of the theology of Structural Sin, which are both explained later.

The Economic Ethos Explanation
Harrison, in *Underdevelopment is a Way of Thinking*[1] developed his proposals based on certain social attitudes, which he believed would lead to economic development. These are portrayed in Figure 2.1.

---

[1] Lawrence E. Harrison, *Underdevelopment is a State of Mind* (Lanham, MD: The Center for International Affairs, Harvard University and University Press of America, 1985).

Figure 2.1
Harrison's What Makes Development Happen[2]

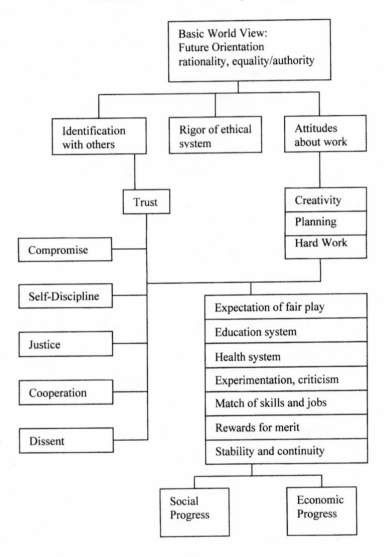

---

[2] Ibid., 5.

These attitudes led to seven critical factors, which are (1) an expectation of fair play, (2) an educational system that provides basic skills, promotes problem-solving and nurtures inquisitiveness, creativity and critical thinking, (3) a good health care system, (4) an environment that encourages experimentation and criticism, (5) freedom to match skills, desires and jobs, (6) rewards for merit and achievement, and (7) political and social stability and continuity.[3] But note, in Harrison's view, it is these attitudes that lead to the critical factors of development, not necessarily the society's implementation of these attitudes.

Yasumasa Tanaka has a similar view and model. He argues for the importance of the "subjective," or "non-material," culture as the source for the "Policy-Making Machinery," which "is centrally responsible for planning, deciding, and executing modernization."[4] Although both institutional and psychological factors appear in the figure, Tanaka argues that the subjective culture, or psychological factors, is

> more important because it is the source of any problem of social, economic and political significance, local or global, or past, present or future. . . . Secondly, economic and industrial development, or modernization, must first take place in subjective culture. Subjective culture is the prime-mover of change and development.[5]

Harrison supported his argument with a survey of other authors who, according to him, share similar views (Gunner Myrdal, W. Arthur Lewis, Max Weber, Joseph A. Schumpeter, David C. McClelland, Gabriel A. Almond, Sidney Verba, Edward C. Banfield and Carlos Rangel) and a series of comparisons (Nicaragua with Costa Rica, Dominican Republic with Haiti, Barbados with Haiti, Argentina with Australia) which suggested that although the innate economic possibilities of each pair are comparable, the vast difference in current economic status can be traced to Hispanic heritage. His little quiz in Chapter 7, entitled "Spain and Spanish America," "suggests the close parallel between recent Spanish history and Spanish-American history."[6] He concluded the chapter thus:

---

[3] Ibid.,5.

[4] Yasumasa Tanaka, "A Cross-Cultural Social-Psychological Approach to Socio-Economic Development," *Managerial Psychology* 4, no. 1 and 2 (1983): 16-17.

[5] Ibid., 21.

[6] Harrison, *Underdevelopment*, 132.

While it is well ahead of the countries of Hispanic America in most key indicators of human progress, Spain is well behind the democracies of Western Europe and North America, Australia, and Japan. What has stood in Spain's way? What we have seen in this chapter strongly suggest that its failure to build a viable and stable political system with which most Spaniards could identify has been a decisive factor. That failure has been accompanied by chronic political upheaval or the oppressive stability of dictatorship. The former has been highly discouraging to entrepreneurial activity; growth has occurred in the latter, but it has resulted in benefits markedly skewed toward the upper strata of Spanish society . . . I believe Spanish America's failure to keep pace with North America is also principally explained by the same cultural factors.[7]

Harrison's argument sounded like the put down that the author frequently heard Brazilians express about themselves—"What do you expect from the descendents of a bunch of no account bums—Portuguese outcasts, African slaves and wild Indians?" How could they compare with the "New-Model Man" of Adam Smith, Alexis de Tocqueville, Benjamin Franklin and others described in Ralph Lerner's article, "Commerce and Character: The Anglo-American as New-Model Man?"[8]

Other authors, such as Michael Novak and Carlos Rangel, and institutions, such as the American Enterprise Institute for Public Policy Research, followed similar lines of thought, criticizing Latin American expectations that they say inhibit economic development in those countries. Novak, though Catholic himself, especially attacked the influence of the Catholic Church in Latin America. Archbishop Marcos McGrath, while weighing his argument towards the Structural Sin explanation of poverty, freely pointed out, "The contribution of the church to [economic] development is a vision we share and a vision we try to incarnate into the realities that affect us all."[9]

---

[7] Ibid., 147-48.

[8] Ralph Lerner, "Commerce and Character: The Anglo-American as a New-Model Man," in *Liberation South, Liberation North*, ed. Michael Novak (Washington, D.C.: American Enterprise Institute for Public Policy Research, 1981), 24.

[9] Marcos McGrath, "The Role of the Catholic Church in Latin American Development," in *Latin America: Dependency or Interdependence?* ed. Michael Novak and Michael P. Jackson (Washington D.C.: American Enterprise Institute for Public Policy Research, 1985), 117.

Table 2.1
Economic Ethos Pattern

1. Not have "Traits that lead to wealth"
    a. worldview - future orientation, rationality, equality
    b. relation with others (rigorous ethics)—cooperation, compromise,
        self-discipline, justice, dissent
    c. work attitudes - creativity, planning, hard work

2. Not have Weberian Protestant Work Ethic
    a. worldly success may be God's reward
    b. all vocations are sacred, so work to please God
    c. individual is competent to make own judgment
    d. having a savings is worth doing without
    e. hard work is a virtue
    f. contemplative life is not step above working

3. "Negative Catholic influences:
    a. anti-capitalism
    b. emphasize social harmony in oppressive political system
    c. anti-liberal society, anti-individualism
    d. anti-industrialization"

4. "Negative elements of Latin American culture:
    a. excessive egoism
    b. excessive dignidad and machismo
    c. excessive concern with status
    d. disdain for manual labor
    e. apathy, lack of commitment, withdrawal
    f. belief in getting ahead through "pull" or trickery
    g. institutionalized corruption
    h. loyalty to family and patrons vs. loyalty to law
    i. absence of civic culture
    j. paternalistic, autocratic entrepreneur
    k. high power distance"

Sources: Drawn from Harrison 1985, 5, 116, 132; Kim 1977, 257-8;
Novak 1982, 286,324-5; McGann 1966, 102-3, 110-3; Nida 1974, 9;
Hofstede 1984:90.

Gustavo Gutierrez pointed out the Catholic Church's tendency to emphasize social harmony over justice.[10] Novak's argument was that although Spain and Portugal were at one time most important and powerful nations on earth, they didn't understand why that was so and eventually lost their power due to the slow integration of church and state. Now, according to Novak, the Latin American bishops claimed that they are victims of capitalism without owning up to three hundred years of Catholic hostility to capitalism. Thus, anti-capitalist ideology preached for all those years has simply produced its fruit.[11]

Modernization

Literature on change and the developmental school of international economics are also examples of this explanation for poverty since both emphasize economic growth through modernization and adoption of technology, or as Jacques Ellul puts it, "technique is regarded in advance as the only solution to collective problems (unemployment, Third World misery, pollution, war) or individual problems."[12] *Culture Matters*, edited by Harrison and Huntington, is the most important new book on the subject.[13] Such negative views of "traditional societies" form a part of the presuppositions for "Change Theory" literature such as Rogers and Shoemaker's Communication of Innovations.[14] Bermant and Warwick began to make this presupposition explicit by bringing up the ethical considerations of "the politics of defining the disadvantaged as victims of social illness."[15]

Some Religious Versions of the Economic Ethos Explanation

During the last few decades, some fundamentalist and evangelical Christians have begun exerting political pressure. While the early focus

---

[10] Joseph Ramos, "Reflections on Gustavo Gutierrez's Theology of Liberation," in *Liberation South, Liberation North*, ed. Michael Novak (Washington D.C.: American Enterprise Institute for Public Policy Research, 1981), 56.

[11] Michael Novak, *O Espírito do Capitalismo Democrático*, trans. by Helio Polvora (Rio de Janeiro: Nordica, 1982), 324-25.

[12] Jacques Ellul, *The Technological Bluff* (Grand Rapids: Eerdmans, 1990), xvi.

[13] Lawrence E. Harrison and Samuel P. Huntington, ed., *Culture Matters* (New York: Basic Books, 2000).

[14] Everett M. Rogers and F. Floyd Shoemaker, *The Communication of Innovations*, 2nd. ed. (New York: Free Press, 1971), 103, 110.

[15] Gordon Bermant and Donald P. Warwick, "The Ethics of Social Intervention," in *The Planning of Change*, 4th ed., ed. Warren G. Bennis, Kenneth D. Benne, and Robert Chin (New York: Holt, Rinehart and Winston: 1985), 452.

was on church / state relations and traditional topics of morality such as abortion and sex education, more attention is now focused on the morality of the welfare program. Much of the current argument against welfare is laced with references to "going back to the way things were in the past" and seem to represent longing for the civil religion of the 1950s. For this reason, these arguments can be classified as emphasizing the social over the personal and the way of thinking (worldview, values) over the way of acting and, therefore, represent the economic ethos explanation. Prominent authors in this area are discussed later as neo-conservatives in the theology literature review.

Economic Ethos Explanation Presupposed

Beyond those who argue for the Economic Ethos explanation or for the civil religion of the 1950s, many others seem to have assumed such presuppositions, although they have left them unstated. Though not discussing economics, Eugene Nida, in *Understanding Latin Americans*, summarized the descriptions of Latin personality made by the Latin American authors Samuel Ramos, Maria Elvira Bermudez and Rogelio Diaz Guerrero. These descriptions, which included traits like sense of inferiority, opposition to manual labor, fatalism and irresponsibility, described the type of society that, according to Harrison, will not succeed economically.[16]

Geert Hofstede was another who was peripherally arguing economic matters, but hinted at this argument through his discussion of high power distance countries. The figure by Triandis and others demonstrated that among high power distance societies (almost all less developed countries) the common views were that the antecedent of power is "wrestling," the consequence of power is "cruelty," and the antecedents of wealth are "inheritance, ancestral property, high interest charges, stinginess, crime, deceit, and theft."[17] Thus, some would argue that these countries' ethos would have to change in order to modernize, because as it now exists, the only roads to wealth are through inheritance or some form of theft.

Similar to this is Lipset and Lenz' discussion of the effect of perceived corruption on economic growth. Perceived widespread corruption has negative effects on economics, education, and economic inequality; in fact "the wealthy and most economically developed

[16] Eugene A. Nida, *Understanding Latin Americans* (South Pasadena: William Carey Library, 1974), 9.
[17] Geert Hofstede, *Culture's Consequence*, abridged ed. (Beverly Hills: SAGE Publications, 1984), 90.

countries are the least politically corrupt."[18] World Bank research has shown that corruption interferes with education, health-care, cooperative markets and delivery systems.[19]

[18] Seymour M. Lipset and Gabriel S. Lenz, "Corruption, Culture and Markets," in *Culture Matters,* ed. Lawrence E. Harrison and Samuel P. Huntington (New York: Basic Books, 2000), 115.

[19] Deepa Narayan, Raj Patel, Kai Schafft, Anne Rademacher and Sarah Koch-Schulte, *Can Anyone Hear Us?* Voices of the Poor Series (New York: Oxford University Press, 2000), 93.

CHAPTER 3
PERSONAL IRRESPONSIBILITY

This is explanation that the author grew up with, and is probably common in the United States. It is based on the "common wisdom" of the North American people that is also expressed in the "neo-liberal agenda."[1] Although these authors don't discuss economics, this "common wisdom" is evident in studies such as Edward Stewart's American Cultural Patterns and the surveys in Herbert McClosky and John Zaller's The American Ethos.[2] To some degree, this explanation represents what Thomas Sowell calls "the constrained view of man."[3]

These references already point out this explanation's relationship with the Economic Ethos explanation for poverty. The Personal Irresponsibility explanation is in fact the ethos as it relates to the individual. While dependent on the society's ethos, it is independent of it in this study since this explanation is (1) highly individualistic and (2) is highly oriented toward behavior. This explanation is how one person would live out society's ethos. Thus, it is the person's actions that cause or don't cause poverty in this explanation, not the whole society's worldview and values. This is what separates it from the Ethos explanation.

Its basic point is that people are poor because they are irresponsible—make mistakes of judgment, get themselves in jams, are injured through carelessness, etc. Some point out that alcoholism, too

---

[1] Ida Susser, preface to The New Poverty Studies, ed. Judith Goode and Jeff Maskovsky (New York: New York University Press, 2001), viii.

[2] Edward C. Stewart, American Cultural Patterns (Yarmouth, ME: Intercultural Press, 1972), 64-68; Herbert McClosky and John Zaller, The American Ethos (Cambridge: Harvard University Press, 1985), 81.

[3] Thomas Sowell, A Conflict of Visions (New York: William Morrow and Co., 1987), 19-23.

many children and marital mistakes contribute to poverty.[4] The critical point is that these people "knew better," yet took irresponsible chances, or even "chose to do wrong."

This explanation is often implicit in the instructions given to the poor on how to change. Sorokin lists family, school, church and occupation as channels out of poverty,[5] but it may come out sounding like "pay attention to your family and honor it, stay in school and study hard, go to church and be good, find a good job which can lead to a career and work hard—in other words, be like me!"[6] This explanation implies that there is something pathological about the individual, his thinking and behavior, which could be repaired if he would simply imitate good folks!

According to Adam Smith, the logic and foundation of this view probably comes from the working class' own experience.[7]

> The vices of levity are always ruinous to the common people, and a single week's thoughtlessness and dissipation is often sufficient to undo a poor workman for ever, and to drive him through despair upon committing the most enormous crimes. The wiser and better sort of the common people, therefore, have always the utmost abhorrence and detestation of such excesses, which their experience tells them are so immediately fatal to people of their condition.[8]

While Smith refers to the "wiser and better sort of the common people," given the predominance of the middle class and its rise from poverty in one generation (from 1930s to post World War II), this abhorrence of "thoughtlessness and dissipation" is easily assumed to be both a working class and middle class value in the United States now.

These descriptions of the explanation that places the blame for poverty on one's own irresponsibility can be summarized as in Table 3.1.

---

[4] Richard P. Coleman and Lee Rainwater, *Social Standing in America* (New York: Basic Books, 1978), 234-36.

[5] Pitirim A. Sorokin, *Social and Cultural Mobility* (London: Free Press, 1927), 183-97.

[6] See also Stewart, *American Patterns*, 64.

[7] Marxist thought would likely say this is ideology.

[8] Adam Smith, *The Wealth of Nations*, Modern Library ed., ed. Edwin Canaan (New York: Random House, 1937), 746.

Table 3.1
Personal Irresponsibility Pattern

1. Little importance given to education
    a. not finish high school
2. Often marry young
    b. have children young before able to support
    c. "too many" children
3. Not "good employees"
    a. lazy
    b. often late
    c. misses work often
    d. not productive
    e. problems with other employees
    f. quits easily
    g. changes jobs often
    h. works seasonally
4. Unwise use of money
    a. gambling
    b. vices
    c. in debt
    d. not invest
5. Not care for health
    a. problem in hygiene
    b. poor nutrition
6. Selfish

Sources: Drawn from Sowell (1987), Stewart (1972),
McClosky and Zaller (1985), Sorokin (1927) and Coleman
and Rainwater (1978).

CHAPTER 4
DEPENDENCY THEORY

The fourth explanation for poverty could be called Dependency Theory or Structural Sin. The first is the secular economic theory; the second is its theological correlation. Dependency Theory is based on Lenin's development of Marxism and argues that the poverty of poor countries is caused by oppression by rich countries.

Roots of Dependency Theory

Marx contributed three theses to this explanation. First, society is determined by the mode of production. Contrary to Weber, Marx attested that the social consciousness, which has an almost over-whelming control of the consciousness of the individual, is rooted in the society's economic organization. Second, poverty of the worker is caused by the owner's expropriation of the surplus produced by the worker. In other words, the owners hoard everything beyond what is needed to maintain the worker alive and productive. Third, the owners dominate the political structure and ideology (the ideals espoused by the society which are never reached, but encourage the continuation of the status quo) in order to maintain their power. Through the ideology, the educational system, family life, views of property and even the ecclesiastical system all contribute to the maintenance of the owner's wealth.[1]

Lenin developed this class conflict to include national conflict in his Theory of Imperialism. Thus, the wealthy nations expropriate all of the surplus produced by the poor nations and control the political and ideological systems.

---

[1] Dennis Gilbert and Joseph A. Kahl, *The American Class Structure*, 3rd ed. (Chicago: Dorsey Press, 1982), 3-4.

Dependency Theory

Dependency Theory applies this to today's "Third World countries." The so-called "developed nations" control the "developing nations," often through the developing nation's own political system.[2] International corporations are usually the agents that oppressively control the national economy even while creating enclaves of well-being through paying their own employees wages higher than the national average. But dependency theorists insist that the overall result of these international corporations is to limit the economic activity and keep prices of raw materials and labor very low. They expropriate the wealth through the exportation of raw materials at prices controlled by the industrialized nations,[3] the restriction of land ownership in the developing nation,[4] the control of the internal industry of the developing nation by international corporations, control of foreign capital and technology[5] and the huge international debts of the developing nations.[6] This view can be summarized as in Table 4.1.

The Trilateral Commission is the central figure in the second phase of the Dependency Theory. It was founded in the early 1970's by David Rockefeller and united over 200 of the leading political, industrial and financial leaders of the U.S., Europe and Japan.[7] And the result of this greater integration of power will surely be greater poverty and greater repression of the poor by their governments.[8]

This interpretation of international economic relations is so well known that it is reflected in fiction novels. Jorge Amado gives a fictional account of the expropriation of cacau plantations by foreigners in

---

[2] Jorge Pixley and Clodovis Boff, *Opcão Pelos Pobres* (Petrópolis, Brazil: Vozes, 1986), 31.

[3] Lucio Kowanick, *Capitalismo e Marginalidade na América Latina*, 4th ed. (Rio de Janeiro: Paz e Terra: 1985), 69.

[4] Fernando H. Cardoso, *Política e Desenvolvimento em Sociedades Dependentes*, 2nd ed. (Rio de Janeiro: Zahar, 1978), 69-71.

[5] Ibid., 210-211.

[6] Ibid., 211; Ronaldo H. Chilcote and Joel C. Edelstein, *Latin America: Capitalist and Socialist Perspectives of Development and Underdevelopment*, Latin American Perspectives series, no. 3 (London: Westview Press), 51.

[7] Alberto Micheo, "O Caso Carter," in *A Trilateral: Nova Fase do Capitalismo Mundial* ed. Hugo Assmann, trans. Hugo P. Boff, 3rd ed. (Petrópolis, Brazil: Vozes, 1986), 19-20.

[8] Franz J. Hinkelammert, "O Credo Economico da Commissao Trilateral," in *A Trilateral: Nova Fase do Capitalismo Mundial* ed. Hugo Assmann, trans. Hugo P. Boff, 3rd ed. (Petrópolis, Brazil: Vozes, 1986), 94-103.

São Jorge dos Ilhéus, as Hess does about bananas in *From the Other's Point of View.*[9]

Table 4.1
Dependency Theory Pattern

1. International Trade Relations
    a. foreign corporate domination of local politics
    b. exports only raw material
    c. imports almost exclusively manufactured goods
    d. foreign control of land ownership
    e. foreign corporate control of national manufacturing
    f. foreign corporate control of technology
    g. heavy national debt controlled by foreign entities

2. National Social Structures
    a. prevalence of hierarchical personal relationships
    b. racism
    c. poor health structures
    d. ideologizing mass media
    e. poor, unavailable or "weeding out" educational system

2. National Economic Structures
    a. low minimum wage
    b. "glass ceilings" in careers (education, social class)

3. National Political Systems
    a. hierarchical relations
    b. inefficient bureaucracy
    c. personalism in politics
    d. inaccessible, non-democratic structures

Social Sin

Clodovis Boff defines social or structural sin as "a human evil that acquires an existence exterior to the individual and imposes itself on the consciousness of the individual."[10] The unjust structures of the

---

[9] Jorge Amado, *São Jorge dos Ilhéus* (São Paulo, Brazil: Círculo do Livro), 130-134; Daniel J. Hess, *The Other's Point of View* (Scottsdale, PA: Herald Press, 1980), 86-117.

[10] Clodovis Boff, "O Pecado Social," *Revista Ecclesiastica Brasileira* 37 (1977): 693; similar definition in Arthur Rich, "Imperativos Objetivos de la Economía y Pecado Estrutural," trans. and condensed Carlos Gonzalez, *Selecciones de Teologia* 24 (January-March 1985): 37. Translations from Portuguese and Spanish throughout this book are by Michael Landon.

society are to the society what lust is to the individual. Moser explains that structural sin is perpetuated in the society through "means, models, ideas, values, the collective mentality."[11]

Prominent liberation theologians are passionate in their repeated linking poverty with injustice, oppression, idolatry and even death.

> The poor is the sub-product of the system in which we live and for which we are responsible. He is the marginalized from our social and cultural world. Even more, the poor is the oppressed, the exploited, the proletariat, the one deprived of the fruit of his work, the one plundered of his humanness.[12]

> The poor are poor because they are exploited or rejected by a perverse economic organization, as in our capitalism. This is the exploitative and exclusive system. For this very reason, the poor is oppressed and suffers. He is maintained under the system or out of it. Such is the true explanation of the poverty of the poor.[13]

> It deals first of all with an alternative in which in the name of some divinities, explicit religiously or in secularized visions such as "democracy," "private property" and national security," death is given to men, dehumanizing them and impoverishing them.[14]

> The current ruling structures, dependent capitalism and national security, . . . act as true gods and as their own worship . . . And they have their own worship because they demand daily sacrifices of the majorities and the violent sacrifice of those who fight against them. This deity has the necessity of victims to subsist and produces them by necessity.[15]

Criticism of Dependency Theory and Social Sin

Most of the criticisms of Dependency Theory have been economic, but Landon has done some research as well on the social presuppositions of Social Sin.

---

[11] Antonio Moser, "Pecado e Condicionamentos Humanos," in *Grande Sinal 1975* (Petrópolis, Brazil: Vozes, 1975), 346.

[12] Gustavo Gutierrez, *Teologia da Libertação*, 6th ed. (Petrópolis, Brazil: Vozes, 1986), 256.

[13] Jorge Pixley and Clodovis Boff, *Opção Pelos Pobres* (Petrópolis, Brazil: Vozes, 1986), 21.

[14] Jon Sobrino, *Ressurreição da Verdadeira Igreja* (São Paulo, Brazil: Edições Loyola, 1982), 155.

[15] Ibid., 173.

Economic Criticisms

The literature on dependency theory is based on empirical macro-economic data, but the theorists have been continually criticized for less than precise work. Often, even the theoretical pieces seem to be more rhetorical than empirical. Cardoso, in the appendix to his well-known book, *Politica e Desenvolvimento em Sociedades Dependentes* (Politics and Development in Dependent Societies), admits that his data was not scientifically sufficient. "Between a rigor that would lead to paralysis and a flexibility which would deliver positive results, we decided on the second alternative."[16]

Ramos says that the economic data does not support Dependency Theory. The U.S. has only made five percent of its international investment in Latin America and the after tax return is approximately ten percent. This does not explain the U.S.'s wealth or Latin American poverty.[17]

Moll calls for the end of Liberation Theology's dependence on dependency theory because it is so weak. He criticizes both the failure of the predictive power dependency theory and methodological weakness. Dependency theory predicts: (a) increasing poverty in the "periphery" nations, (b) increasing inequality between the "center" and "periphery" nations, and (c) increasing world inequality, but the first two are not occurring.[18]

According to Moll, the methodological contradiction is that Lenin (his theory of imperialism is the basis for dependency theory) admitted that capitalism is productive and progressive, as least for the productive forces within the society. Thus, even to Lenin, capitalism is a useful bridge to socialism.[19]

McCann criticizes the lack of precise economic data in the arguments both for and against Dependency Theory. He attempts to clarify the situation through a few case studies on international corporations. He cites competing descriptions of the same situation in Lernoux's *Cry of the People* and Williams and Houck's *Full Value*, but even these seem more theory-laden than precise.[20] These case studies however, are

---

[16] Fernando H. Cardoso, *Politica e Desenvolvimento em Sociedades Dependentes*, 2nd ed. (Rio de Janeiro: R.J.: Zahar, 1978), 210.

[17] Dennis P. McCann, "Liberation and the Multinationals," *Theology Today* 41 #1 (April 1984): 52-3.

[18] Peter Moll, "Liberating Liberation Theology: To Independence from Dependency Theory," *Journal of Theology for Southern Africa* no. 78 (1992): 29-33.

[19] Ibid., 34.

[20] McCann, "Multinationals," 56-7.

macro-economic studies of multinational corporations, not the micro-economic study of family units.

Criticisms of Social Sin's Presuppositions

Landon has criticized the social presuppositions of Social Sin's version of Dependency Theory. He relates these six major presuppositions: 1) social evolution operates so that 2) economics (mode of production) and 3) dialectical materialism (class conflict) determine the major features of the society, which 4) creates religion to support the dominant classes and 5) takes on an existence exterior to individuals that 6) largely determines the individual. In other words, the individual has practically no choice in participating in an evil, oppressive economic system.[21]

These presuppositions are largely Marxist, with a sprinkling of Durkheim.[22] Weber held contrasting views on causality in society—he believed economics, society and religion were mutually influencing each other, with perhaps religious ideas exerting the strongest influence.[23]

Conclusion

Liberation theologians took Dependency Theory and called it sin—sin of the social structures, as is presented in the theology section later. Thus, in this explanation of poverty, the pathology is in the larger society, not the poor. The poor are poor because they are victims of the oppression of the society, but especially the worldwide economic system.

---

[21] Michael L. Landon, "The Social Presuppositions of Early Liberation Theology," *Restoration Quarterly* 47 (2005): 17-28.

[22] Ibid.

[23] Max Weber, *The Protestant Ethic and the Spirit of Capitalism,* trans. Talcott Parsons (New York: Charles Scribner's Sons, 1958), 183.

CHAPTER 5
U.S. ADAPTATIONS OF
CULTURE OF POVERTY

While the four explanations for poverty presented above have tended to operate on the international discussion of poverty, only one has been influential among researchers in the United States. While there is a structural explanation for poverty among U.S. researchers, and it is the dominant argument among sociologists and social workers, it seems to have no influence from or on Dependency Theory. The Culture of Poverty explanation, however, has been influential in the United States.

The argument in North American has tended to center on "culture-vs-structure dichotomies."[1] On the "culture" end are those arguments that emphasize the thinking and behavior of the poor as the cause of poverty. Of those, the best known is the Culture of Poverty, which according to Corcoran, has evolved into four different explanations under the general title of "intergenerational transmission of poverty."[2]

Corcoran summarized the four intergenerational transmission of poverty explanations in her article, "Rags to Rags." She called them the "Material Resources" model, "Correlated Disadvantages" or "Human Resources" model, the "Welfare Culture" model and the "Underclass" model.[3]

---

[1] M[ary] Corcoran, "Rags to Rags: Poverty and Mobility in the United States," *Annual Review of Sociology* 21 (1996): 242; Judith Goode and Jeff Maskovsky, introduction to *The New Poverty Studies,* ed. Judith Goode and Jeff Maskovsky (New York: New York University Press, 2001), 10-13.
[2] Corcoran, "Rags to Rags," 242.
[3] Ibid., 242-45.

These four explanations of intergenerational poverty are presented first, and then the next chapter presents another two common theories in the U.S. are presented: a structural argument and the Stress model. After these two parts, the last chapter of this section presents the comparison of these six explanations and how they relate to the four international explanations above.

The Human Resources Model

This explanation was the closest to the original Culture of Poverty explanation. Its basic premise was that poverty was transmitted from generation to generation through faulty characteristics of the family. Less education on the part of the parents may have made them "less effective in developing of their children's human capital."[4] The family structure effect was based on the fact that "poor families are more likely to be headed by a female" and may have included "reduced parental supervision" and "the absence of good role models for work and marriage."[5] The third factor that Corcaran mentioned was that "genetically based intelligence differences fuel intergenerational poverty and dependency."[6]

This last factor, which was hotly debated a few years ago, pointed to some of the authors that have contributed to this explanation. Prominent authors mentioned by Corcoran and others include Haveman, Wolfe, Spalding, Becker, McLanahan, Sandefur, Hernstein and Murray.[7] Fagan from the Heritage Foundation has several papers in the area, as well. The most hotly debated was Hernstein and Murray's *The Bell Curve* which simply established the high corrolation between the kind of intelligence typically measured on college entrance exams or

---

[4] Ibid., 243.

[5] Ibid; Patrick F. Fagan, "How Broken Families Rob Children of Their Chances for Future Prosperity," Heritage Foundation paper #1283 (1999) available at www.heritage.org/research.

[6] Corcoran, "Rags to Rags," 243.

[7] R. Haveman, B. Wolfe, and J. Spalding, "Childhood Events and Circumstances Influencing High School Completion," *Demography* 28, no. 1 (1991): 133-47; Gary S. Becker, *A Treatise on the Family,* enlarged ed. (Chicago: University of Chicago Press, 1991); S. S. McLanahan and G. D. Sandefur, *Uncertain Childhood, Uncertain Furture* (Cambridge: Harvard University Press, 1994); Richard J. Hernstein and Charles Murray, *The Bell Curve: Intelligence and Class Structure in American Life*, Free Press Paperback ed. (New York: Simon and Schuster, 1994).

IQ tests and later income and the high corrolation between test scores and ethnicity, among other things.[8]

Harris' article on women, work and welfare gave further details of the human capital explanation for poverty. First, the socioeconomic circumstances of the woman's family of origin influenced her likelihood of leaving welfare for work. "Welfare mothers who have lived with both her parents most of their lives and whose mothers have acheived at least a high school educations, for instance, are expected to have shorter stays on welfare."[9]

Table 5.1
Human Resources Pattern

1. Little education by parents leads to less developed children
    a. mother without high school education
2. Female headed families
    a. lived with one parent most of life
    b. age and time as female head of household develop coping techniques
3. Genetic IQ Disadvantage
4. Race
5. Certain life events
    a. early childbearing limits education and work
6. Socio-economic context
    a. labor market conditions
    b. amount of welfare received

Sources: Drawn from Corcoran 1995 and Harris 1993.

Second, although controversial and unexplained, race was a factor. "Black women have been found to experience more persistence on welfare."[10] Third, "certain life-course events" have been found to be influential. Early childbearing jeopardized work, as well as single mothers who never marry. Age and time spent as a head of the family should improve her performance.[11] This explanation can be summarized as in Table 5.1.

---

[8] Hernstein and Murray, *The Bell Curve*, 91-142, 269-315.
[9] Kathleen M. Harris, "Work and Welfare Among Single Mothers in Poverty," *American Journal of Sociology* 99, no. 2 (1993): 323.
[10] Ibid.
[11] Ibid., 323-24.

The Welfare Culture Model

The Welfare Culture model, like the earlier Culture of Poverty model, emphasizes deviant values, attidudes, and behaviors, but contends that these values, attitudes and behaviors are fueled by the government welfare system.[12]

The difference between this model and that of the Culture of Poverty explanation was that this model made it clear that the negative attitudes and behaviors were the results of receiving welfare, not causal factors of poverty. While the Culture of Poverty model, as it has been used, seemed to blame the poor, the Welfare Culture model blamed the government for entrapping the poor in poverty and dependency.

Corcoran provided the details of this argument. According to the welfare culture argument, when parents and neighbors rely heavily on welfare, the stigma associated with being on welfare disappears; parents and neighbors develop self-defeating work attitudes and poor work ethics; and these attitudes are passed on to their children. In addition, parental welfare recipiency provides children with poor role models for work and marriage. Girls raised in welfare-dependent homes and communities are more likely to drop out of high school, to have illegitimate births, and to go on welfare themselves. Boys raised in welfare-dependent homes and communities are more likely to grow up to father children out of wedlock, to drop out of high school, to hang out, to engage in crime, and avoid regular work.[13] Fagan also proposes that "welfare harms kids," but concentrates on the increase in illegitimate births among welfare girls.[14]

This explanation for poverty is largely dependent on Mead.[15] His central point was that government programs to help the poor have failed not because they gave too much or too little, but because they "have been permissive, not authoritative."[16] This was because of the libertarian nature of American politics.[17]

---

[12] Corcoran, "Rags to Rags," 244.

[13] Ibid.

[14] Patrick F. Fagan, "How Welfare Harms Kids," Heritage Foundation paper #1088 (1996) available at www.heritage.org/research.

[15] Lawrence M. Mead, *Beyond Entitlement*, (New York: Free Press, 1986); Lawrence M. Mead, *The New Politics of Poverty*, (New York: Basic Books, 1992).

[16] Mead, *Beyond Entitlement*, 1.

[17] Ibid.

Table 5.2
Welfare Culture Pattern

1. Stigma of welfare disappears, no incentive to play by rules (work,
   marry, etc.)
2. Self-defeating work attitudes and work ethics
3. Poor role models for work and marriage
4. Welfare girls
   a. dropout school
   b. illegitimate children
   c. go on welfare
5. Welfare boys
   a. illegitimate births
   b. drop out school
   c. crime
   d. avoid work
6. racism

Sources: Drawn from Corcoran (1995); Mead (1986, 1992) and
Murray (1984).

"The goal must be to create for recipients *inside* the welfare state
the same balance of support and expectation that other Americans face
outside it, as they work to support themselves and meet the other
demands of society."[18] Murray, the same one mentioned above in the
Human Resources explanation for poverty, concurs with Mead's as-
sessment. "Welfare rewards those who don't play by the rules (i.e. who
have children out of wedlock and do not work) and penalize those who
do play by the rules."[19] Murray's solution is to do away with welfare, at
least the subsidizing of illegitimate births, something recommended in
The Bell Curve, as well.[20]

The Material Resources Model
This explanation returned to the family as the cause of the
transmission of poverty from one generation to the next. The Human
Resources Model focused on characteristics of the family such as
education, family structure and inherited intelligence. This model was

---

[18] Ibid., 4 (emphasis Mead's).
[19] Corcoran, "Rags to Rags," 245.
[20] Charles Murray, *Losing Ground*, Tenth-Anniversary ed. (New York: Basic
Books, 1994), xvi-xvii; Hernstein and Murray, *The Bell Curve*, 548-49.

similar since it centered on the family, but shifted the focus to the material resources of the family.

This lack of material resources included the lack of income to invest in the education of the children, the lack of time, money or energy to devote to develop the children, fewer networks for finding jobs and living in poorer neighborhoods which likely means lower quality schools, fewer good role models, less social control, fewer job markets and more likelihood of gangs and crime.[21] See Table 5.3.

While Becker included the Human Resources Model in his work, he also made that point that the inheritability of characteristics is also dependent on material resources.

> Indeed, if all parents can readily borrow to finance the optimal investments in children, the degree of intergenerational mobility in earnings essentially would equal the inheritability of endowments.
>
> Poor families often have difficulty financing investments in children, because loans to supplement their limited resoures are not readily available when human capital is the collateral. Such capital-market restrictions lower investments in children from poorer families.[22]

The difference between the Human Resources Model and the Material Resources Model was most evident in the common solutions to poverty based on each model. The followers of the Human Resource

Table 5.3
Material Resources Pattern

1. Demands of survival prevent investment in human capital (mainly schooling)
2. Little supervision of children
3. Poor network to find job
4. Live in a poor neighborhood
   a. poorer schools
   b. less social control
   c. fewer role models
   d. more crime and gangs

Sources: Drawn from Corcoran (1995)

---

[21] Corcoran, "Rags to Rags," 242-43.

[22] Gary S. Becker, *A Treatise on the Family*, enlarged ed. (Cambridge: Harvard University Press, 1991), 272.

or Welfare Culture Model may have recommended encouraging fewer births among the poor by reducing welfare.[23] The proponents of the Material Resources Model would recommend increasing the economic resources of the poor, through welfare, other forms of aid or compensation.[24]

The Underclass Model

The Underclass explanation for poverty provided the key movement in poverty research for the 1990's and was the most commonly used term.[25] It returned to the relationship of the poor with society as the cause for poverty. The poor being considered here were not individuals or families, but poor neighborhoods. According to Corcoran, Wilson asserted that the loss of well paying manufacturing jobs and the migration of the black middle class to the suburbs "reduce the chances of the remaining impoverished residents and their children of escaping poverty."[26]

Wilson said that as long as the middle class and working blacks all lived close by and formed a community, "their very presence provided stability to inner-city neighborhoods and reinforced and perpetuated mainstream patterns of norms and behavior."[27] The current social isolation of poor blacks in urban centers (but not poor whites since they often participate more widely in society) resulted in (1) fewer jobs and higher unemployment, especially among males, (2) which resulted in fewer marriages and more single mother families, (3) weakened social institutions such as churches, and (4) lower expectations from life.[28] Thus, while this model was built on the intergenerational transmission of poverty and continued its "pathological" view of the poor, the focus was on society's role in it.[29] This explanation for poverty can be summarized as in Figure 5.4.

---

[23] Murray, *Losing Ground*, xvi-xvii; Hernstein and Murray, *The Bell Curve*, 548-49.

[24] J. E. Rosenbaum, "Black Pioneers," *Housing Policy Debate* 2: 1179-1213, reference in Corcoran, "Rags to Rags," 237-67.

[25] Corcoran, "Rags to Rags," 246; Christopher Shea, *The Chronicle of Higher Education* 4 October (1996): A12-13.

[26] Corcoran, "Rags to Rags," 245.

[27] William J. Wilson, *The Truly Disadvantaged* (Chicago: University of Chicago Press, 1987), 7.

[28] Corcoran, "Rags to Rags," 245-46.

[29] Goode and Maskovsky, "Introduction," 12.

Figure 5.4
Underclass Pattern

1. Fewer good jobs leads to higher unemployment
2. Fewer employed men leads to fewer marriages
3. Weakened social institutions (churches, political parties)
4. Lower expectations from life

Sources: Drawn from Corcoran (1995)

As economic and social situations change, cultural traits, created by previous situations, likewise *eventually* change even though it is possible that some will linger on and influence behavior for a period of time. Accordingly, the key conclusion from a public policy perspective is that programs created to alleviate poverty, joblessness, and related forms of social dislocation should place primary focus on changing the social and economic situations, not the cultural traits, of the ghetto underclass.[30]

In a later inteview, Wilson said, "I was out in the field, looking at the notes and listening to people, and it wasn't poverty that was coming up—it was jobs, jobs, jobs."[31]

Conclusion

These four explanations for poverty above all accepted the intergenerational transmission of poverty, but differed as to the source and cause. The Human Resources and Material Resources explanations focused on the family as the source and mechanism of transmission of poverty.

The Welfare Culture and Underclass explanations focused on a subset of society in and through which poverty is transmitted (those who receive welfare, or ghetto neighborhoods), but placed the cause on the action of the larger society through a permissive welfare system or social isolation.

---

[30] Wilson, *Truly Disadvantaged*, 138 (emphasis Wilson's).
[31] Shea, *Higher Education*, A12.

CHAPTER 6
U.S. STRUCTURAL PROBLEMS

The fifth explanation for poverty among the U.S. theories is a structural argument that focused on the difficulties of earning a sustainable income in the U.S., especially by single mothers. Much literature has been produced along these lines, but great collections are in a special issue of the *American Journal of Orthopsychiatry* (October 1996) and *New Poverty Studies* by Goode and Maskovsky.[1] This special edition of *AJO* was prompted by the recent changes in the welfare laws, and the authors made clear their bias.

> Not surprisingly, the reality of poor women's lives was also ignored. In creating this special issure, we hoped to inject a note of reality into the discourse about welfare. By bringing together researchers, teachers, and clinicians—all of whom had worked with women on welfare—we sought to give voice to a feminist view of the real needs of poor families and the real solutions to a public welfare system gone awry.[2]

Goode and Maskovsky also made clear their perspective.

> The essays collected here, however, are collected for the purpose of advancing the argument that poverty is a direct outgrowth of uneven capitalist development; . . . these essays focus on the complexity of

---

[1] Judith Goode and Jeff Maskovsky, Introduction to *The New Poverty Studies,* ed. Judith Goode and Jeff Maskovsky (New York: New York University Press, 2001).

[2] Amy Salomon, "Welfare Reform and the Real Lives of Poor Women," *American Journal of Orthopsychiatry* 66, no. 4 (1996): 486.

power relations through which poverty is produced, maintained, and reconfigured.[3]

This explanation argues that poverty is caused by the larger society that finds poverty useful for maintaining it own dominance and wealth. According to this explanation, poverty is maintained through unjust jobs and welfare system, lack of adequate structures to meet family needs of the poor, and the resulting stress and violence.

Jobs

The main body of what this author has dubbed the U.S. Structural Problems explanation for poverty dealt with the difficulties of getting and keeping jobs and other forms of income. "Structural variables (i.e. factors that exist independent of any particular individual) such as lack of jobs, hours and wages of jobs, and lack of available child-care options, provide the context for unemployment."[4] Not only were the jobs often not available, but they usually included low wages, non-daytime shifts, part-time work and lack of benefits such as vacation, medical insurance or paid sick leave.[5] A similar problem is lack of reliable transportation to and from work.[6]

Family Needs

"In the present study, the limited supply of affordable child care was the greatest barrier to employment for women".[7] Besides regular childcare, because of the poor health of many welfare recipients, additional needs included family leave time and flexible hours.[8]

---

[3] Goode and Maskovsky, "Introduction," 17.

[4] Margaret G. Brooks, and John C. Buckner, "Work and Welfare: Job Histories, Barriers to Employment, and Predictors of Work among Low-Income Single Mothers," *American Journal of Orthopsychiatry* 66, no. 4 (October 1996): 527.

[5] Chaya S. Piotrkowski, and Susan Kessler-Sklar, "Welfare Reform and Access to Family-Supportive Benefits in the Workplace," *American Journal of Orthopsychiatry* 66, no. 4 (October 1996): 539.

[6] Stephanie Aaronson, and Heidi Hartmann, "Reform, not Rhetoric: A Critique of Welface Policy and Charting of New Directions," *American Journal of Orthopsychiatry* 66, no. 4 (October 1996): 585.

[7] Brooks and Buckner, "Work and Welfare," 534.

[8] Piotrkowski and Kessler-Sklar, "Welfare Reform," 539.

Table 6.1
U.S. Structural Problems

1. Problems with jobs
    a. not available
    b. part-time jobs
    c. low minimum wage
    d. no or few benefits, health care
    e. poor hours–not enough hours or evening shift
    f. no transportation
2. Family needs not met
    a. childcare
    b. family leave time
    c. safety
    d. flexible hours
3. Welfare system
    a. benefits too low
    b. humiliating
    c. limited for two parent families
4. Psycho-social victims of violence
    a. stress
    b. been in foster care
    c. mentally ill

Drawn from Salomon 1996; Piotrkowski and Kessler-Sklar 1996; Salomon, Bussak, Brooks 1996; Withorn 1996; Brooks and Buchman 1996.

Because of the violence discussed above, these women need to take safety as an important consideration for their family.[9]

Welfare

The welfare system was strongly criticized by these authors. Withorn and Sidel asserted that it is just as "wrong" or "right" for a woman to be dependent on welfare as for a woman to be dependent on a man, her husband.[10] Because welfare came to be perceived as for the

---

[9] Amy Salomon, Shari S. Bassuk, and Margaret G. Brooks, "Patterns of Welfare Use among Poor and Homeless Women," *American Journal of Orthopsychiatry* 66, no. 4 (October 1996): 513-14.

[10] Ann Withorn, "'Why do they hate me so much?' A History of Welfare and its Abandonment in the United States," *American Journal of Orthopsychiatry* 66, no. 4 (October 1996): 505; Ruth Sidel, "The Enemy Within: A

undeserving poor, unlike Social Security, the experience became both humiliating and coercive.[11]

Given that welfare is limited for two adult families and "it makes more sense for vulnerable women to stay home with their children and help them navigate the drug- and crime-plagued environment,"[12] these goals were set for government policy by Aaronson and Hartmann:

> Within this context, we have devised the following policy goals: 1) to provide a social safety net for all Americans; 2) to lift single women and their families out of poverty; 3) to enable women and their children to live in a safe, supportive environment; 4) to enable women to earn a living for themselves and their families; and 5) to integrate poor women and their families into society.[13]

Their policy recommendations included: (1) "increase the minimum wage further, expand the income and child-care tax credits," (2) "provide paid family and disability leave," (3) "expand unemployment insurance (UI) to cover more part-time and low-earning workers," (5) "ensure universal access to health insurance," (6) "improved quality child care to families that need it," (7) "allow women to retain more of their assets and income from outside sources" (continue receiving welfare when begin working), (8) "increase child-support payments."[14]

The Demonization of the Welfare Mother

The most poignant part of the issue were the articles by Sidel, Withorn and Schnitzer on the "demonization" of welfare mothers. Schnitzer pointed out that the stories told about welfare mothers in the health clinic paralleled the national stories or views of poverty: (1) "They don't come in" (they are irresponsible), (2) "They're so disorganized" (they are cognitively incompetent) and (3) "They don't care" (they are morally defiant).[15]

Commentary on the Demonization of Difference," *American Journal of Orthopsychiatry* 66, no. 4 (October 1996): 491.

[11] Withorn, "History of Welfare," 498-99.

[12] Ibid., 497, 504.

[13] Aaronson and Hartmann, "Reform, not Rhetoric," 583.

[14] Ibid., 587-91.

[15] Phoebe K. Schnitzer, "'They don't come in!' Stories Told, Lessons Taught about Poor Familes in Therapy," *American Journal of Orthopsychiatry* 66, no. 4 (October 1996): 576.

Schnitzer and others affirmed that these stories did not take into account the difficulties these poor single mothers were having in just surviving. She reviewed the "stress model," which simply showed that "economic hardship and child cognitive development and emotional and conduct difficulties" correlate.[16] Brooks and Buckner and others also pointed out the extremely high incidence of violence on welfare mothers. [17]

The alarming rates of violence in the entire sample cannot be overlooked. Overall, 85.3% of respondents were victims of severe physical violence, sexual assult, or molestation during childhood and adulthood.[18]

---

[16] Ibid., 578.

[17] Salomon, Bassuk, and Brooks, "Patterns of Welfare Use," 517-18.

[18] E. L. Bassuk, L. F. Weinreb, J. C. Buckner, A. Browne, A. Salomon, and S. S. Bassuk, "The Characteristics and Needs of Sheltered Homeless and Low-Income Housed Mothers," *Journal of the American Medical Association* 276 (1996) cited in Brooks and Buckner, "Work and Welfare," 535.

CHAPTER 7
STRESS MODEL

The Stress Model was referred to in the discussion above on the structural explanation for poverty. It is derived from literature on stress and literature on homelessness.

Stress and Poverty

Kleinman seems to have been the first to use the term "stress model."[1] McCloyd summarizes the model thus: (1) parental distress in the form of anxiety, depression and irritability, (2) which resulted in inappropriate disciplinary techiques which were punitive, erratic, unilateral and unsupportive, such as nagging, scolding, ridiculing and threatening, (3) which tended to increase the inappropriate behavior by the child.[2]

A part of the stress model is the violence that often accompanies poverty. Shipler writes

> The ten year old girl sat on an idle swing, chatting with the caseworker on the swing beside her. "How many times," the girl asked, "have you been raped?"
>
> The question came casually, as if it could merely glide into the conversation. The caseworker, "Barbara," tried to stay composed.
>
> "I said that I hadn't, and she was surprised," Barbara recalled.

---

[1] Arthur Kleinman, *Rethinking Psychiatry* (New York: Free Press, 1988), 63.

[2] V. C. McCloyd, "The Impact of Economic Hardship on Black Families and Children," *Child Development* 61 (1990): 311-46, quoted in Phoebe K. Schnitzer, "'They don't come in!' Stories Told, Lessons Taught about Poor Familes in Therapy," *American Journal of Orthopsychiatry* 66, no. 4 (October 1996): 578.

"'I thought everyone had been,'" she remembered the girl saying.
    "Her friends talked about it in school," Barbara observed. "It's
an everyday thing."[3]

Shipler reports that twelve out of the thirteen boys and girls that
Barbara worked with had been sexually molested and "a surprising
number of women at the edge of poverty turn out to be survivors of
sexual abuse."[4] Salomon, Bassuk and Brooks also pointed out the
extremely high incidence of violence to welfare mothers.[5] The alarming
rates of violence in the entire sample cannot be overlooked. Overall,
85.3% of respondents were victims of severe physical violence, sexual
assult, or molestation during childhood and adulthood.[6] Shipler goes on
to argue that "trauma debilitates in ways consistent with handicaps
frequently seen among the poor," such as helplessness, capacity for
intimacy as adults and unhealthy parternships, dissociation, and early
sexual involvement. Sexual abuse affects the poor differently than the
wealthier since it is a "pileup of multiple stresses."[7]
    International sources also report that depression, stress, lack of
self-esteem and violence are common among the world's poor.[8]
    Hauser disputes these conclusions, however, by calling for not just
corrolations, but causal links between economic hardship and increased
psychological problems,[9] because most of the research seemed to

---

[3] David K. Shipler, *The Working Poor*, Vintage Book ed. (New York: Vintage
Books, 2005), 142.

[4] Ibid., 142-3.

[5] Amy Salomon, Shari S. Bassuk, and Margaret G. Brooks, "Patterns of Welfare Use Among Poor and Homeless Women" *American Journal of Orthopsychiatry* 66 #4 (October 1996): 517-18.

[6] E. L. Bassuk, L. F. Weinreb, J. C. Buckner, A. Browne, A. Salomon, and S.
S. Bassuk, "The Characteristics and Needs of Sheltered Homeless and Low-
Income Housed Mothers" *Journal of the American Medical Association* 276
(1996), cited in Margaret G. Brooks and John C. Buckner, "Work and Welfare," *American Journal of Orthopsychiatry* 66 #4 (October 1996): 535.

[7] Shipler, *Working Poor*, 142-3.

[8] Deepa Narayan, Robert Chambers, Meera Kaul Shah, and Patti Petesh, *Crying Out for Change*, Voices of the Poor Series (New York: Oxford University
Press, 2000), 93-5, 119-31.

[9] Stuart Hauser, "Finding the Causal Links," *Public Health Reports* 111 (1996).

simply establish the corrolation.[10] Kleinman also warned again excessive dependence on the stress model since

> increasingly, contemporary society medicalizes social problems. Alcoholism, once a sin or moral weakness, is now a disorder. . . . The same is true of drug abuse, certain kinds of truancy and delinquency for which children and parents were once held legally responsible to school authorities but which are now relabeled as conduct disorder, and a wide range of the experienced problems of daily living, now called stress syndromes, which to a greater or lesser degree have biological antecedents, correlates, and consequents.
>
> Medicalization—whether seemingly scientifically justified or not—is an alternative form of social control, inasmuch as medical institutions come to replace legal, religious, and other other community institutions as the arbiters of behavior. . . . For example, Stone (1984) has shown that the American disability system has come to medicalize problems of poverty, under- and unemployment, and worker alienation.[11]

The Homeless

In the literature on homelessness, there was a much stronger causal argument. Whether stress was originally caused by society's oppression or not, the resulting stress caused poverty. Roberts and Keefe identified five types of homeless people, one of which is the "mentally disor-dered." This category included the "schizophrenic," "alcoholic," "alcoholic schizophrenic."[12] These people came to be homeless because of the limited federal benefits for mental hospitalization, extended federal benefits available for housing them in nonpsychiatric homes, and mandated "least restrictive setting" for treatment of mental patients.[13] Snyder and Hombs report in the section entitled "Paths to Poverty" that

---

[10] Jane D. McLeod, "Contextual Determinants of Children's Responses to Poverty," *Social Forces* 73 (1995): 1487-516; Margaret E. Esnminger, "Welfare and Psychological Distress," *Journal of Health and Social Behavior* 36 (1995): 346-59; Pamela K. Klebanov, Jeanne Brooks-Gunn and Greg J. Duncan, "Does Neighborhood and Family Poverty Affect Mothers' Parenting, Mental Health, and Social Support?" *Journal of Marriage and the Family* 56 (1994): 441-55.

[11] Kleinman, *Rethinking Psychiatry*, 9.

[12] Ron E. Roberts and Thomas Keefe, "Homelessness," *Journal of Sociology and Social Welfare* 13 (1986): 403.

[13] Roberts and Keefe, 404.

the careless and wholesale depopulation of the nation's mental hospitals has resulted in deinstitutionalizing former patients to the streets or, if they are "lucky" to shelters with insufficent services instead of to community care facilities. The American Psychiatric Association estimates that 1 million or more homeless people in our nation are desperately in need of mental health care.[14]

Lamb and Talbott report that about 40% of the homeless have a major mental illness.[15] Lyon-Callo points out that this has become the major explanation for homelessness in the U.S. He said that shelters assume this model and encourage the guests to reflect until they find the "biological disorder, an attitude toward life, mental illness, a lack of self-discipline, or an addictive personality" that explains their situation.[16]

How do they become homeless? It began with the wholesale deinstitutionalization of the mentally ill, which they don't think was bad per se, but did not place the mentally ill in adequate community programs.

Once on their own, they often can not deal with "even ordinary landlord-tenant situations," much less more difficult ones, or jobs.[17] Many drift away out of boredom, or they may be trying to escape to drink or use drugs. Often they stop taking medication regularly and lose touch with the Social Security Administration. "They may now be too disorganized to extricate themselves from living on the streets."[18] These explanations can be summarized as in Table 7.1.

Kozol disputes the claim that most of the homeless were homeless because of severe mental illness because he believed it to be a way to avoid the other issues, such as cost of housing and low income, which

---

[14] Mitch Snider, and Mary E. Hombs, "Homelessness is Serious," in *The Homeless: Opposing Viewpoints*, ed. Lisa Orr, Opposing Viewpoints Series, ed. David L. Bender and Bruno Leone (San Diego: Greenhaven Press, 1990), 18.

[15] Richard H. Lamb, and John A. Talbott, "Mental Illness Causes Homelessness," in *The Homeless: Opposing Viewpoints*, ed. Lisa Orr, Opposing Viewpoints Series, ed. David L. Bender and Bruno Leone (San Diego: Greenhaven Press, 1990), 56.

[16] Vincent Lyon-Callo, "Homelessness, Employment, and Structural Violence," in *The New Poverty Studies,* ed. Judith Goode and Jeff Maskovsky (New York: New York University Press, 2001), 302-3.

[17] Lamb and Talbott, "Mental Illness," 57-58 and Shipler, *Working Poor,* 121-3.

[18] Lamb and Talbott, "Mental Illness," 57-58.

are more difficult to deal with. He does admit, however, that "a certain number of the homeless are or have been mentally ill".[19] Lyon-Callo also claims that the cause of homelessness is current economic structures, especially the declining wages of many workers.[20]

Table 7.1
Stress Pattern

1. Stress
    a. difficult economic conditions
    b. parental distress
        1) anxiety, 2) depression, 3) irritability
    c. inappropriate discipline techniques
        1) punitive, 2) erratic, 3) unilateral
        4) unsupportive, 5) nagging, 6) scolding
        7) ridiculing, 8) threatening
    d. inappropriate child behavior
2. Homeless
    a. schizophrenic
    b. alcoholic schizophrenic
    c. marginality
    d. misfortune
    e. mental disfunction
    f. alcoholic

Sources: drawn from Schnitzer 1996: 578; Kleinman 1988: 63; McCloyd 1990: 330-1; Roberts and Keef 1986, 403-7.

Conclusion
Regardless of the incidence of mentally ill homeless people, the Stress Model of poverty composed of literature corrolating financial hardship and mental illness and the literature attributing homelessness to psychological illness is an explanation for poverty in the United States.

---

[19] Jonathan Kozol, "Mental Illness Does Not Cause Homelessness," in *The Homeless: Opposing Viewpoints*, ed. Lisa Orr, Opposing Viewpoints Series, ed. David L. Bender and Bruno Leone (San Diego: Greenhaven Press, 1990), 61.
[20] Lyon-Callo, "Homelessness," 308.

CHAPTER 8
SUMMARY OF EXPERTS' EXPLANATIONS

In Figure 0.1 above, the four international explanations for poverty were arranged on a grid composed of two continuums: individual / social and ways of acting / ways of thinking. The six explanations for pov-erty operating in the United States also fit on that grid, as seen in Figure 8.1.

The Grid of Explanations for Poverty

As explained earlier, the grid is divided between those explana-tions for poverty that emphasize ways of thinking and those that em-phasize the ways of acting and also those that emphasize that the poor themselves, a sub-group, or the larger society is the cause of poverty. Added to the Ways of Thinking side of the grid from the U. S. explanations for poverty discussion above are the Stress Model, Human Resources and Welfare Culture explanations. The Stress Model centered on the individual and one's psychological well being, a way of thinking argument, and fits in that spot on the grid.

Figure 8.1
Fitting the Expert's Explanations Together

	Personal Cause	Sub-group Cause		Structural Cause
Thinking	Stress	Culture of Poverty	Welfare	Economic Ethos
Acting	Personal Irresponsibility	Material Resources	Underclass	Structural Sin

The Human Resource explanation fits in the same spot as the Culture of Poverty explanation since it centered on the family and what the parents could pass onto the children through I.Q., nurturing and contacts. The Welfare Culture explanation dealt with a subset of the American society, those that receive welfare, and it explained poverty as a way of thinking imposed by the welfare system.

On the bottom side of the grid are the explanations that emphasize ways of acting. Added to the two previous explanations are the Material Resources, Underclass and U.S. Structural Problems explanations. The Material Resources explanation emphasized the family and how its financial resources influenced the development of the children, so it fit under the Culture of Poverty explanation.

The Underclass explanation emphasized a subset of the larger society, the ghetto neighborhood, and how its social isolation led to the depletion of community norms, role models and resources for higher income, so it fits on the soical side, as a subset of society. The U.S. Structural Problems explanation for poverty was very similar to and fit in the same category as the Structural Sin explanation.

Cultural Systems and Social Systems
There are numerous displines that study humans,[1] but they differ in methods and emphases. As Corcoran mentioned, the causes of poverty tend to be explained in cultural versus structural arguments.[2] In Figure 8.1 above, there is a tendency to identify the ways of thinking end of the continuum with cultural systems and the ways of acting end with social systems. The differences between and overlapping areas of cultural systems and social systems are discussed by Parson in several texts,[3] but this grid, however, helps one to be a little more precise.

Cultural anthropology, even when it studies ways of acting, has a tendency to emphasize ways of thinking (the meanings and understandings) in the person that accompany those actions.[4] But cultural anthropology also it tends to center on the actions and interactions of individuals and small group, not large modern societies. Thus, cultural

---

[1] Paul G. Hiebert, *Cultural Anthropology*, 2nd ed. (Grand Rapids: Baker Book House, 1983), 20-25.

[2] M[ary] Corcoran, "Rags to Rags: Poverty and Mobility in the United States," *Annual Review of* Sociology 21 (1996): 242.

[3] Talcott Parsons, *The System of Modern Societies* (Englewood Cliffs, NJ: Prentice-Hall, 1971), 4-6.

[4] Hiebert, *Cultural Anthropology*, 25-29.

studies would tend to focus on the upper, left side of the grid including the Culture of Poverty, Human Resources, Welfare Culture, Individual Irresponsibility and Material Resources explanations for Poverty. Cultural Anthropology would share that upper, left side of the grid with psychological studies, as demonstrated by the Stress Model.

Sociology, however, tends to center on studies of large, modern groups. It tends to center on social systems, which include second level social interactions. The first level social interactions tend to be face to face and are studied more by anthropologists and psychologists, while these second level social interactions tend not to be face to face. They include social institutions, economic and political structures and others.[5] Thus, social systems would center on the lower, right side of the grid, including Welfare Culture, Economic Ethos, Material Resources, Underclass, Social Sin and U.S. Social Problems explanations for poverty.

Conclusion
Ten explanations for poverty were discovered in the literature and presented here. They are compared and put on two continuums, a ways of thinking versus ways of acting continuum and an individual versus social continuum, based on their assumptions or assertions to two fundamental questions: is poverty caused by improper thinking or by improper actions and is poverty caused by the poor themselves or by society as a whole?

What is remarkable about many of these explanations is how they tend to concentrate on one or two major factors as the causes of poverty and tend to apply that explanation to all low income people. Perhaps, it is a rhetorical device of exaggeration, but it does offend many low income people, and I think it does not help the discussion. The reader will see how the media portrayals of poor people affects many in the following section. And personally, I desire more practicality, reason and service and less theory, blustering and empire-building.

---

[5] Antonio Moser, "Mais Desafios para a Teologia do Pecado," *Revista Eclesiástica Brasileira* 40 (December 1980): 684.

SECTION II
WHAT LOWER INCOME ADULTS SAY
CAUSES POVERTY

This section presents and analyzes what six low-income adults said causes poverty. The first chapter briefly describes the town where they lived—Hammond, Louisiana. The following five chapters contain their comments, based primarily on my written observations of visits and transcripts of the three taped interviews which I did with each informant (called the Life History Interview, Causal Differentiation Interview, and the Card Sorting and Ranking Interview).

Each one's explanation is contextualized by a description of his or her home and a brief life history. Each one's explanation for poverty is also briefly compared with the ten theories from the literature review. Of course, to protect their anonymity, names and identifying data have been changed.

The last chapter compares their explanations for poverty with each other and with the 10 explanations from the experts.

CHAPTER 9
THE CONTEXT OF HAMMOND, LOUISIANA

By most standards, Hammond is a relatively small town since its population is about 16,000. Although not the parish seat, Hammond is the largest town in the parish and is surrounded by smaller towns within five to ten miles, the largest of which is Ponchatoula with 6,000 residents.

Hammond has a long tradition of dairy business and truck farming, especially strawberries. The berries were grown in nearby fields, taken to huge warehouses in Hammond where they were sold to buyers from Chicago and shipped by railroad all over the country. Hammond was also home to the Zemurray family, founder of Standard Fruit Company that I believe became a part of United Fruit Company, which was later accused of abuses of power in Central America.[1] Although the family has died out, its memory continues in the area's two major parks, Zemurray Park and Zemurray Gardens.

Hammond is now a bedroom community for many middle class employees of the chemical and petroleum industry about 45 minutes away. It is home to the fastest growing university in the United States, Southeastern Louisiana University, with about 13,000 students. Although many students commute from Baton Rouge and other areas, the university supports many faculty and staff in Hammond, and the commuting students boost the service industry of the town.

---

[1] Penny Lernoux, *Cry of the People* (Garden City, N.Y.: Doubleday, 1980), 115-19.

Economic Status

Despite these many economic boosts, the per capita income of Hammond is less the parish average, which is less than the state average, which is less than the national average. According to the 1990 Census, 25.1% of the families and 31.5% of the individuals in Tangipahoa parish lived at poverty level or less, while 28.6% of the families and 38.3% of the individuals of Hammond lived at poverty level or less.[2] Also, 64.8% of the households in the parish earned $24,999 or less per year.[3]

Urbanicity

While Hammond is definitely not a large city, it does have something of the feeling of an urban area. Although it is not an industrial center, it is the commercial center for the parish and at the same time has a concentration of poverty. Gangs and violence also attract media attention. The schools are avoided by the middle class by living in nearby school districts or using private schools. There is an identified housing area known as "the projects."

Ethnicity

The largest ethnic groups are the "whites" (57%) and "blacks" (42%), with less than 1% Spanish Americans or Asians.[4] Although there are various subgroups in nearby parishes (e.g., Catholic families with backgrounds from Italy and "Cajuns" of French descent) these are not significant to this area.

Migration

Little recent migration has taken place in Hammond. In 1990, almost 50% of households had lived in the same residence five years earlier. Most of the changes in residence occurred in the same town and

---

[2] U.S. Department of the Commerce 1993, p. 10, 530; 1990 Census of Population, Social and Economic Characteristics: Louisiana, p. 10, available at http://www.census.gov/prod/cen1990/cp2/cp-2-20-1.pdf.

[3] U.S. Department of the Commerce 1994, p. 246; 1990 Census of Population, Social and Economic Characteristics: Louisiana, p. 276, available at http://www.census.gov/prod/cen1990/cp2/cp-2-20-1.pdf.

[4] U.S. Department of the Commerce 1993, p. 542; 1990 Census of Population, Social and Economic Characteristics: Louisiana, p. 28, available at http://www.census.gov/prod/cen1990/cp2/cp-2-20-1.pdf.

less than 5% had moved from out of state.[5] The "new immigrants" mentioned above seem to be almost entirely middle class families transferred to this region.

---

[5] U.S. Department of the Commerce 1993, p. 500; 1990 Census of Population, Social and Economic Characteristics: Louisiana, p. 2, available at http://www.census.gov/prod/cen1990/cp2/cp-2-20-1.pdf.

CHAPTER 10
BOB AND CARLA'S STORY

Bob is married to Carla, both African-American. Bob doesn't strike me as fat, but he does have a protruding stomach reminiscent of the potbelly of malnourished children in Africa. They have three children: a teenaged girl in high school, another girl about 10 years old and a son who is preschool. I think Carla already had the first two children when she met Bob. Although Bob had problems in school, both Bob and Carla completed eleventh grade, but not the twelfth.

MLL: You went to school here in Hammond?
Bob: Yah, I went to school in Hammond. I went all the way up to the 12th in the Special Education Class. Just because the people said I was evil, because the way I talk. They said it wasn't the right way, but I had some people come back and say that was the right, but that was too late they put me in special ed.

I had trouble understanding the speech of everyone in the house, but his speech didn't seem more difficult than most of the others. Carla and my research assistant often interpreted for other members, but sometimes when I would ask later what someone had said, the black research assistant would say that she didn't understand it either.

Although Carla did receive AFDC, food stamps and a subsidized housing, both she and Bob worked in short spurts in the food service industry several times during the two years I visited them. Plus, I eventually figured out that Bob often worked short-term day or week manual labor jobs during most of that time.

Bob said, "Working, single, everything was alright." Bob had worked in the food service industry as a teenager, continued in that sector when he moved out of state to work for several years and back again in Hammond. When he first moved back to Hammond, he first worked on a construction crew which closed down because the boss's drug habit, and was cheated out of his wage, and then at a lumber mill where he had an accident in one of their vehicles and was fired. He also had tried to make money selling soft drinks and using his stepbrother's car as a taxi, both of which were shut down by authorities.

Bob and Carla's Home

Bob and Carla live in a ragged house near the "projects." It has a short gravel and mud driveway, where there were commonly neighbors' two or three cars parked on the driveway and front lawn. There were several trees nearby so I tried to stay out of the mud by walking on the leaves and gravel. There was a large (1 foot wide by 2 feet long by 1 foot deep) rut or pothole in the middle of the driveway.

The house was about 20 feet by 3 feet or maybe 1000 square feet or less with a green clapboard exterior and some white trim with traces of mildew. These 1000 square feet included a screened in porch in the front and another in the back. The roof was bumpy, covered with little branches and leaves. We entered the porch through a wood frame screen door. The porch had several things in it, but wasn't crowded. Along the path to the front door of the house was an empty five-gallon bucket. I don't know what it was for.

Bob and Carla's home had four bedrooms, which were taken advantage of by his extended family. For the first year I knew them, they had his parents and two cousins living with him. Later, the owner of the house forced the extra family members to leave. The condition of the house changed when the extended family left. While they were still there, I would frequently encounter the following situation.

As I entered the house, I notice a strong smell. I don't know what it is, since it is not food or a spice, but I think it is caused by a lack of airing out. It is the smell I've smelled before in very poor homes. The grandfather is smoking. As I stay for a while, the first odor is no longer so noticeable, but the smoke bothers me.

There are clothes and food packages & bottles everywhere! The food is not prepared food, but the packages (i.e., package of cookies opened and half eaten, big cylinder container of salt, boxes of prepared food). I notice several brand name products, such as French's mustard; I remember xxx talking about how food stamps were too many to feed the family, so people have to trade for cash to pay utilities. I also notice a huge 20-pound sack of sugar on the kitchen counter (it had a label, I don't remember what it was, but it wasn't a government looking label). Food containers also are scattered all over the kitchen counters & stove. The kitchen table also had a pile of mail, mostly bills, lying open on the table—that reminded me of my own home.

The grandfather has an ash trey on the couch beside him, but cigarette stubs are also scattered about on the table and floor. I thought it strange to see three cigarette butts together on the table, with a few black ashes scattered around them. The floor also has plenty of pieces of paper. The TV was turned on fairly loud and remained on during my visit. It made it harder for me to understand.

The extended family didn't seem to be a good influence, as demonstrated by this visit by local drug dealers while I was present.

I noticed the police car going by on the main street. The group of young men slowly moved to the playground in the center of the square, sat for a while and then came to the porch where we were. We sat in silence watching them. (And I looked around so as to not be staring. I wished that I could be invisible, but it's hard to blend in when I'm the only white guy in the area. I did keep thinking that it was great to be able to just sit and watch and listen.)

I noticed that the young men would frequently look toward us, but never all at the same time or stare for a long time. One of them had a Dallas Cowboy coat, but otherwise their dress was nondescript.

As they arrived at the foot of the stairs, one of them greeted me, "Hi" or something like that and I returned the greeting. They talked a lot, mainly with each other and with a woman or two from the nearest house. One of the young men goes next door and returns a few minutes later talking about "she's going to fuck my ass." He repeats this several times.

Bob gets up and talks with them several times, each time for less than a minute. One of them says something about "she" and "fifty." He replies something about "her check." The dialogue is not aggressive, but very brief. And then he returns to sit down. Once he goes to the door of the apartment and says something to someone inside, but I don't know to whom or what he said. Bob's sister came out briefly, and stood on the porch saying that she had to dress her mother because she was the only one who could do it. Then she went back inside. It's all rather amazing because of the silence of Bob and his friend. I don't know if it is because of the young men, the recent death of Carla's sister or what.

Most of young men went next door for a few minutes, although some stayed near the porch we were on. I didn't look to see if they were looking at us. I asked Bob quietly if they were wanting money from his sister. He said, "Yes, they say a hundred and a half." I reply that I had heard something about "fifty." I asked if they were friends, or if they loaned money as a business. Bob said that they were drug dealers.

When they returned to the porch, they're still talking, as they had been since they arrived. One of them was saying, "she said she has AIDS here and HIV here," motioning first to his left chest and then to his right chest and laughing as he talked.

After the extended family left, the house was cleaner and quieter.

As I entered, I had difficulty seeing since it was dark as compared to the outside. I recognized Carla sitting in a recliner on my left, facing toward the TV, but I recognized her because she leaned over to see me. There were three girls sitting on a sofa and Bob was laying on a love seat, all watching TV.

The furniture was all different than my previous visits. The recliner was tan. The sofa and loveseat were black vinyl, and I sat in the matching chair. The coffee table was the same, but the TV appeared to be different (newer design) and it was sitting on a small nightstand type table in the corner, with the VCR on top of it. There was a small table between me and the TV, but the kitchen table that had occupied the place of the chair was gone. The freezer was still there and in the same place. The room was neat, swept, no ashtrays or paper laying round or on the coffee table. There was also a box fan with one grating missing next to the chair on my right, blowing air toward the loveseat. I noticed no smell, and the temperature was comfortable.

I could see that the kitchen had some boxes of food in it, with some pots boiling, but it looked relatively clean. The worn, mismatched tile in the hall, living room and kitchen was the same. The hall was also swept and free of any boxes or furniture.

The new furniture may have been obtained at a rent-to-own store. Earlier, Bob had gotten Carla a new bedroom set for her anniversary at a rent-to-own store. According to them, everyone did it in their neighborhood. A few months later, Bob asked for a loan to make a week's payment on the set, which I refused. I don't know what happened to the set.

Bob and Carla's Immediate Neighborhood

Across the street, I commonly saw a car with four young African American men sitting on it. (Everyone I've seen in this area is black. Unless otherwise noted, everyone is black except me). The car is sitting at the dead end of the road. There are about six in the group. Music is playing, but not unusually loud. They didn't seem to notice me.

I also regularly saw several young women and children walking or playing in the area. On one occasion, I saw two or three young women sitting in two white lawn chairs with several preschool age children around them and in their lap. They were talking and laughing happily, but I could not understand. They had on nice-looking, cotton white blouses that are kind of long—they fluttered in the slight breeze. As I walked toward Bob and Carla's house, I saw several more children (preschool and school age) about 20 feet away squatting near the road looking at the other group and laughing. I heard someone from the first group saying loudly, "Hit him back!" After hearing it repeated, I turned to look and saw everyone looking at one of the young (2 years old?) children. One was on a tricycle and another the same size was standing nearby. Evidently, one of them had hit the other, and the young women were encouraging the second to hit back, but I didn't know.

Bob's Explanation for Poverty

When I first proposed interviewing them about poverty, Bob and Carla responded with some enthusiasm with comments like that following: "You could write a book about what I have to say;" "Those politicians are all in it for themselves, promising things and then not doing them;" "The story of my life is what you need!;" "Yah, they're cutting welfare, but not providing jobs for people;" "And the minimum wage just doesn't do it!;" "It's got to go up!" Bob said that he had been out of a job for two years, since he had had a wreck in the company vehicle. There was a bit of anger, or at least frustration, in their comments.

They talked freely. They talked about the minimum wage and food stamps—how it wouldn't work. Bob said that Carla is now working at local store, but she never gets 40 hours, usually only 20 hours, so $80 doesn't do much. But it does lower her food stamps! Bob said something about the primary problem is paying rent; they only receive enough money to pay the rent, so families have to sell food stamps to get money to pay for utilities.

Bob constantly referred to the need for job openings! It seemed like he thought jobs were the cure for all our social evils!

I was listen to, about a couple years ago, I was listen to a radio, something on a radio, where the president was asking, "What's the problem?" You know, I be saying to myself, "I need to call him, I can tell him what the problem is, I can stop the situation I think. . . ." Ok, if you want to stop drugs, you need to go in the jail, that where the drugs is. You want to stop drugs. If you want to stop drugs, get them off their butt and get them a job, don't have time. You got people working from ten to ten. You got people work that don't get to see daylight, they don't have time for drugs. Some of them grew up on drugs because they didn't have a job. Got a job working from ten to ten, will get them off that stuff. They won't have time.

They wanted jobs, but complained that they couldn't find them, especially jobs that paid above minimum wage.

Bob: Everybody and special they open up a buncha places and they not even opening up no jobs so people can go out there and get, "Ah, I'm going to call ya."
MLL: What kind of places?
Bob: Places that open up. They be hiring, the paper say they be hiring and you go out there and they not hiring.
Bob: Now they trying to cut off the welfare, best thing you could do, cut off the welfare, open up some job. The ones that want to work there, go get'em and the ones that don't want to work, won't go get'em. I'm not talking about opening up some job at $4.25. No! Nobody can live off $4.25. It should be like any other city, I went to Pennsylvania, minimum wage is $7. Here it $4.25, minimum wage here suppose to be five somethin. Some job still paying $4.25, the job I'm on now making $4.25, that's Trey's Inn.

During the two years I visited them, Bob and Carla didn't keep the jobs they had. Bob quit from one job because the owner asked him to "clean the toilet with his hands," since the brush was broken. Carla was fired from her job after being accused of stealing, which she claimed was just a personal vendetta with another worker, as had happened once before on a different job.

Carla: On racialism, they have people don't like you, they prejudice toward you.
MLL: Like what happen at your last job.
Carla: And the job before that. See like if you haven't been there for a while, and you come there, and the man like the way you doing your work. And then people there don't like it, do anything, you know, to try to get rid of you, and that called racialism.
MLL: So it not necessary racism from your boss, it's other people.
Carla: It's other people, my last job it wasn't my boss, it was somebody else, another supervisor in the store.
MLL: Has it always been whites that has been racialism against you or . . . ?
Carla: No. This here it was a white man working, but it was a black girl that me and her got into it. But she had been there longer than I

was. But see by me, I usually come there and do my work, I didn't talk. I, you know, I didn't be in the group with them. I just be by myself. And so he told me she'd been here longer, that's the way he said it, she was here before he was. He was a white guy; the girl I was into it with was a black girl.

Tables 10.1 and 10.2 show the results of Bob's Card Sorting & Ranking for poverty in general and his own low income. Strangely enough, in his Card Sort and Ranking exercise, Bob continued to strongly emphasize the social causes of poverty, but the importance of a job almost dropped out completely!

Table 10.1.
Causes of Poverty in General According to Bob

Major Causes of Poverty in General
1. Welfare is not enough
2. The Projects
3. Kids having babies
4. School not teach well
5. No or few benefits given at job
6. Having to pay for transportation to job
7. No jobs available
8. Extended family (parents, sister, etc.) need /want help
9. No one helps get a job, no relatives to help get a job
10. Not taught how to work

Minor Causes of Poverty in General
1. Unemployed
2. Minimum wage is too low
3. Pat time wage is too low
4. Not a part of a union
5. Prejudice
6. Churches don't help people
7. TV encourages kids to want too much
8. Not allow (renter to have) home business / personal attack (by owner)
9. Computers take away jobs
10. Other people try to keep down

Not a Cause of Poverty in General
Have to support family; Police and judge don't help; Law doesn't help people; Don't like the way you talk; Bills, debt (rented furniture); Churches/church people are absentee landlords (example—the projects); Don't have long term job; Law interferes in disciplining kids; Cut welfare when get a job

For poverty in general, it dropped to seventh position among the major causes, and for his own situation, it was not included as a factor. What was emphasized was the shortcomings of the welfare system (payments too small, interferes in family life, the atmosphere in the subsidized housing) and the shortcomings of the jobs that were available (low wage, no benefits, no transportation).

Table 10.2
Causes of Bob's Own Low Income

Major Causes of Bob's Own Low Income
1. TV encourages kids to want too much
2. Prejudice
3. The projects
4. Not taught how to work
5. Law interferes in disciplining kids
6. Minimum wage is too low
7. Churches/ church people are absentee landlords (example - the projects)
8. Don't like the way you talk
9. Extended family (parents, sister, etc.) need /want help

Minor Causes of Bob's Own Low Income
1. Other people try to keep down
2. Computers take away jobs
3. Kids having babies
4. Having to pay for transportation to job
5. Not a part of a union
6. School not teach well
7. Have to support family
8. Part time wage is too low
9. Churches don't help people
10. Cut welfare when get a job

Not a Cause of Bob's Own Low Income
No or few benefits given at job; Police and judge don't help; Law doesn't help people; Not allow (renter to have) home business / personal attack (by owner); Bills, debt (rented furniture); Unemployed; Don't have long term job; No jobs available; No one helps get a job, no relatives to help get a job: Welfare is not enough

In the above list of causes of Bob's own poverty, four of the first five things all seemed to indicate ways that the outside was messing with Bob and his family (TV encouraging consumerism, prejudice, the atmosphere of the projects and law interferes with disciplining kids).

Reminded one of the American dream, "a man's home is his castle," which Bob felt was being interfered with by the outside.

Included in this emphasis on the social causes of poverty was Bob's anger at churches, as he expressed on several occasions.

> Bob: Sometimes family don't have grocery in their house, people should be able to help put thing in their house. I think that what the Lord wants.
> MLL: Other ways.
> Bob: Other ways, kids don't have clothes to wear or put on their back. Some kids go in ragged clothes, when you see that you should be able to help them people or go to somebody to help him. Don't just keep him down and leave him there. We got people out there just sleeping in the street. I think the Lord, way he is, he said his house for everybody. My hope, and I'm believing on day, I wish they would open up back the church door and stop locking them and get these people off the street. And stop being demon, the demon way because you have equipment inside your church house. If that's your equipment, take it home with you. Let's open up these doors. The house is the Lord. Maybe we can save somebody.

As quoted above, Bob at one point had declared that welfare ought to be done away with, yet in this final interview, put low payments by welfare as the primary reason for poverty in general, but not at all in his own case! His logic behind this seemed to be very pragmatic, that most people who were in poverty were so because of the welfare system. Yet, he wanted to work and thought that others ought to as well! It was the difficulties associated with getting and keeping a job, to which evidently welfare does not contribute, that most frustrated him personally. Yet, welfare should continue for the benefit of the children of parents who don't want to work.

> They can cut welfare off and open up jobs, and give people jobs. Ones want a job, they have to go out there and get it; the ones who don't, they will suffer. Don't make the kids suffer for the parent. Got to have something for the kids.

Bob did recognize some of the difficulties caused by family and upbringing, but still passed most of the blame to the society for not educating people for jobs.

Summing up Bob's explanation for poverty in the analysis demonstrated in Tables 10.1 and 10.2, Bob's evaluation of the causes of poverty were the second most lopsided of all the informants in reference to both the poor in general and his own low income. Bob's explanation came pretty close to equaling the U.S. Structural Problems explanation for poverty. This is especially interesting since it was written with poor women in focus. When parts of Carla's explanation for poverty is included with Bob's, it strongly reinforces the U.S. Structural Problems explanation for poverty.

Carla's Explanation for Poverty

Carla's explanation for poverty seemed to come right to the point—although she recognized the error of not completing a good education, she placed the major causes of poverty in the realm of the shortcomings of the jobs available, as seen tables 10.3 and 10.4. The job had no childcare system, no benefits, too few hours, too low a wage, no union and racist workers!

Table 10.3
Causes of Poverty in General According to Carla

Major Causes of Poverty in General
1. Not complete education
2. No babysitter to care for children while working
3. Racism
4. Unable to work (no babysitter)

Minor Causes of Poverty
1. Don't get benefits at job
2. Not have a full-time job
3. Minimum wage is too low
4. Not join union / no union available
5. Debt

Not a Reason
Too lazy to work; Have to quit school to take care of sick relative; Early pregnancy and no baby-sitter; Dad use for dependent for income tax; Lose job over personal dispute with other worker; A person's background; High interest on debt

Unlike Bob, who blamed the system for a poor education, Carla blamed herself for her lack of a complete education. In reference to herself, Carla put three of the five major causes of poverty in the realm of individual and family causes, but all of the minor causes were structural, as seen in Tables 10.3 and 10.4. Carla's argument favors mainly structural causes for poverty, but not as strongly as Bob. However, when elements for her structural causes for poverty are included with those from Bob's explanation, it pretty well sums up the U.S. Structural Problems explanation for poverty.

Table 10.4
Causes of Carla's Own Low Income

Major Causes of Carla's Own Low Income
1. Not complete education
2. Not have a full-time job
3. Unable to work (no babysitter)
4. Have to quit school to take care of sick relative
5. High interest on debt / Debt

Minor Causes of Carla's Own Low Income
1. Don't get benefits at job
2. No babysitter to care for children while working
3. Minimum wage is too low
4. Racism/ Lose job over personal dispute with other worker
5. Not join union / no union available

Not a Cause of Carla's Own Low Income
Too lazy to work; Early pregnancy and no baby-sitter; Dad use for dependent for income tax; A person's background

CHAPTER 11
DON'S STORY

Don was a tall (6 feet, two inches, perhaps), slender African American man in his seventies. He dressed in dark colored, older clothes usually. Don's hair had some gray, but not a lot. His wife, Donna, was tall (maybe 5 feet, eight inches) and plump. Her dark hair was short and plastered to her head in short curls. She was friendly, but obviously didn't want to talk with me other than greetings. She refused to be interviewed. Don later told me that she didn't feel worthy to be interviewed since she had only been a housewife and had only about a third grade education.

Don and Donna had 13 children, 52 grandkids and 29 great grandkids. He also mentioned that he had been married to Donna for 57 years, "a long time to be married to one woman," with a grin and no sarcasm. He also said that he never had any problem with the 13 kids, never had to go the police or problems with drugs. He said that he treated the girls like the boys, in bed by 9 P.M. because if there is trouble outside and you don't know where your kids are, what can you do? "People said to treat them differently [the girls]," he said, "but I treated them the same."

The thirteen children included 10 girls and 3 boys. The three boys lived in the neighborhood. The others lived close by except for four girls who lived in other states with their husbands and children. Don and Donna also raised five or six other children of friends or relatives.

He had had a heart attack and stroke at the same time about a year ago. He said that he had worked all his life, whenever he would finish one job, someone would always offer another, and so being sick with nothing to do was really hard. They didn't even let him "turn a wrench hard."

Don was born in 1920 in nearby parish. Donna was born there as well, he said. He was raised on a sharecropping farm and stayed there until about 25 years old. In 1945, he moved to the parish capital where he drove trucks delivering logs to the paper mills. He began as an employee, but when his boss became sick, he bought the truck and worked self-employed.

In 1969, he began to take workers to Michigan to pick crops and did this until a few years ago. Don bought a bus (the old one which still sat beside the house) and signed up at the employment office for workers to take. They picked strawberries, then cherries, apples, then apples, and other fruits.

Don's Home

The house looked from the outside to be about three bedrooms, with good vinyl siding, tan colored I think, with the half to the left on the ground and the half nearest me on cement blocks, with the space uncovered. The windows were covered with screens. The front porch was about 4 feet by 4 feet concrete with concrete steps, which looked good. The porch lead the living room through the doorway, which had a screen door with two 4 inch by 4 inch holes in the screen and a wooden door. Don commented on the flies—there were about twenty flies on the porch, which he said was unusual, but also occurring at his neighbor's. He had washed the porch down several times, but nothing seemed to work. I noticed that the vinyl covering at corner at the porch had broken and a lizard's tail was sticking out of the crack.

Upon entering the house in the living room, I could see the kitchen on the right and a door on the left that led to the bedrooms. During the interviews, Donna stayed in the dining area. Don usually sat on the sagging couch near the stove. Despite the cool Louisiana winter, the room was pleasantly warm, thanks to a wood heater. Don said that this wood stove had worked well for a long time. He got the wood from people who "are always wanting to get rid trees, and one son worked for the city and brought logs." Later, he said that his wife would open the door to the sleeping area, and the stove would heat the whole house.

The walls of the room were covered with pictures, not framed prints or pictures, but just regular developed pictures from a common camera pinned to the wall. There was a group of about twenty-five grouped together on the wall above Don on the couch. There were other such pictures on the other walls, together with other papers, such as a "Mother of the Year" award, probably from one of the children, not an award from an organization. On the wall to my far left, there was a large (24 by 36 inches, perhaps) frame filled with similar pictures.

The TV was on a Sesame Street type show, but the grandchild that Donna babysat never appeared to watch it. Neither did Don. I was probably the only one who noticed it was on.

Don's Explanation for Poverty

Don was "cheated out of an education" as a child, and that dominated his discussion about poverty. He frequently told me how this came about.

> Don: Oh yah, we had school, but we didn't go but about half of the time. And everything I'd like for you to know when we were going to school during that time, we only went about a month and a half out of the whole section. We didn't have but three months to the whole section. But, uh, because of that, the reason was that my daddy was a big farmer, and the boss would ride by, and he and my daddy got along real good. He called him D., his name was xx. And, uh, he would tell my dad, "Now you got a good prospect. I'll tell you what you better do, you better keep the geeses home tomorrow and let them clean the grass out of it." Now the young people have help with it. See in that day and time, we didn't have no help. My dad used say, "You stay here to clean this cotton out or the corn out," and we'd do the choppin. We had plenty of it. And we had to stay there until we got it all cleaned out. If it took three weeks, or the rest of that section.
> MLL: I remember when the first time I came here, you were telling me about that, and you were telling me the geese, that's what they called the . . .
> Don: Yah.
> MLL: kids.
> Don: Because there was a bunch of us at home. So he called us "the geeses." "Keep the geeses home to get this cleaned out. Get this grass out of this cotton and corn." And there wasn't no fuss, there wasn't no hard feelings. You knew just do what he said do, and he would do what the boss said. If he said, "Stay home" to us, we'd get that hoe and get out in that field.

Of course, Don wasn't the only one who was denied an education. In the Causal Differentiation Interview, he mentioned that many were poor because they didn't know how to work, even as late as when he was leading the harvesting crew. He said that since so many people couldn't count, they would put a barrel by the door of the storage bin and every time one brought a load to empty, the worker dropped an ear of corn in the barrel to keep count.

Despite this handicap which prevented Don from ever really advancing a grade or graduating, he was quick to learn. He was helped by relatives who were teachers and taught him mechanics and other useful things by watching, asking questions and doing. Later in life, he took some night courses, but never really got a diploma. He had a girl help him keep books when he led the harvesting crews to Michigan.

People trusted Don, so he was often made a leader among the workers, but he felt the lack of education held him back financially.

> MLL: What, if you had been able to get a better education, what kind of job do you think you would have been able to get?
> Don: Oh well, I would have been in the high bracket police. I'd be working for the police. I was, uh, security guard when they built the Junior High two out on Pine St. over there. . . . Probably eventually people trusted me. I was raised in a big family. My dad was a minister. He taught me to be honest, and I tried to follow along what he taught me. I found out he was good. I raised my kids, thirteen, and I never had any get involved in drugs, or any such thing.
> MLL: That's good! So you think that if you'd gotten a better education, you could have been a policeman, or something else?
> Don: Something else. I think that I probably would have been a leader of the parish. I think that I could have been a leader in the parish. I traveled all over the highways. I knew a whole lot of peoples.

Don knew that this lack of education held him back, but he was unhappy with other things as well, especially the low wages paid.

> MLL: What, uh, were there times when people gave you a hassle, or they let you work for them, or . . .
> Don: Yah, well, . . .
> MLL: Cheated you out of your wages, things like that?
> Don: With wages so cheap, they're cheatin anyway! Uh, they never did pay you full price . . .
> MLL: You said, that, that they already paid so cheap that it was . . .
> Don: Well, it
> MLL: cheatin.
> Don: was as low as it could get! Just made it. Just about as low as you could get, I guess! Because, uh I started out workin, I worked for fifty cents an hour. [He later corrected this to a day's wage.]

As far as the wages were concerned, he found no discrimination. "Uh, it all run about the same thing. . . . Black or white, it was twenty-five cents." Discrimination occurred through the lack of education and limited options for blacks. His father could only farm the poor, "piney woods" areas. And Don was denied jobs because it might have caused a problem to have a black man doing that.

Conclusion

In Don's prioritization of causes for poverty in general, seen in Table 11.1, he gave first priority to the structural problems of low wage and limited access to education, although he reversed the order in which they appeared in the other interviews.

Table 11.1
Causes of Poverty in General According to Don

Major Causes of Poverty in General
1. Extremely low wages
2. Little education, cheated out of education, school not have grades, poor school facilities (no school building)
3. Sit and wait for check from government instead of working, not take opportunities
4. Don't know how to get along with people
5. Give up
6. Racism
7. Try to live big on small wage
8. St. Helena [parish] wages too small
9. Drugs
10. Only allowed to farm poor land (piney woods)
11. Sickness
12. Age discrimination

Minor Causes of Poverty in General
1. Kids live in trailers, but don't pay rent
2. Steal instead of work
3. Smoke
4. Because work was seasonal
5. Young people won't accept learning
6. Politician don't fulfill promises

Not a Cause for Poverty in General
Self doubt; Live in a poor reason; No irrigation for piney woods farm; Don't know what to do, how to work; Not a part of a union; Not trustworthy; Job pay little; social Security is too small; Have to pay rent and utilities; Not use money wisely; Drank wine; Because was good (nice to people) instead of take advantage of workers; Because dad was a sharecropper

When talking about others, Don also gave solid support to the problems that people create for themselves through irresponsible behavior. He listed "Waiting for a check," "No social skills," "Trying to live big on a small wage," "Drugs," and "Stealing." For poverty in general, Don heavily favored acting causes, but gave pretty balanced weight to individual and social causes.

During the Card Sorting and Ranking Interview, Don commented that he was sorting into the Not a Cause pile all the cards that inferred that one was already poor. He only included reasons that would make one poor in his stacks. This action solidly refutes any interest on Don's part in the familial transmission of poverty explanation, as well as some of the details of the structural and other explanations.

Table 11.2
Causes of Don's Own Low Income

Major Causes for Don's Own Low Income
1. Cheated out of an education, made to work; little education, school not have grades, poor school facilities (no school building)
2. Age discrimination
3. Extremely low wages, job pays little, St Helena wages too small
4. Have to pay taxes (corrected "have to pay rent and utilities")

Minor Causes for Don's Own Low Income
1. Racism (comment: in past this was a major reason, but now a minor reason)
2. Because work was seasonal
3. Politicians don't fulfill promises

Not a Cause for Don's Own Low Income
Try to live big on a small wage; Young people won't accept learning; Not use money wisely; Not take opportunities; Kids live in trailers, but don't pay rent; Social Security is too small; Drugs; Live in a poor area; Sit and wait for check from government instead of working; Self doubt; Because was good boss (nice to people) instead of take advantage of workers; Steal instead of work; Smoke; Drink wine; Give up; Don't know how to get along with people; Sickness; Not trustworthy; Not part of a union; Only allowed to farm poor land (piney woods); No irrigation for piney woods farm; Because dad was a sharecropper; Don't know what to do, how to work

When it came to his own low income, however, Don changed drastically. In fact, he was the only informant to negate any personal causes for his own low income. He concentrated exclusively on social and structural causes of poverty, such as "Cheated out of education," "Age discrimination," "Extremely low wages," "Have to pay taxes, rent and utilities," "Racism" and "Politicians lie," as seen in table above. In relation to himself, Don gave the highest concentration of social causes of poverty of all the informants, about 95%. He also gave 100% of the weight to acting causes.

Perhaps a major influence on Don's perception of poverty was the past. When answering my questions and commenting on poverty, Don frequently referred to events from his childhood and early adulthood when racism was rampant and legal. And it's no surprise; the pain of living in such conditions is beyond my comprehension. What was even more remarkable, however, was listening to a man recount personal experiences of such injustice, yet without rancor. Perhaps anger at times, but not revenge. I learned from all my informants, but Don was one of the greatest teachers.

CHAPTER 12
EVELYN'S STORY

Evelyn is a short round woman, a round face and a round body. She is one of those women who has a combination of short arms and big breasts, so when she folds her arms, they rest on her breasts. Eve dressed nicely, such as a nice looking tan blouse with a printed or woven design, with double layers of material in certain sections. It looked like it was made of linen and could be casual or a dressier casual depending on accessories, of which I noticed none.

About her birth, she says,

> I was what you call an accidental experiment. My mother was a cheerleader; my father was a football player, and after their homecoming game, here I am.

Since her parents never married, and her mother continued having other children, Evelyn was raised by a childless aunt and uncle. She and her aunt were faithful church goers.

> I guess I credit that to my aunt, too, cause all I did was go to church. We went, um, sung in the choir, and taught vocational Bible School and different things like that.

Her uncle drank too much, and that caused problems during the early years, but he always worked and supported them.

> When I went to kindergarten, we were living in, this little, it was like a little three, four room little shack. Uh, he would . . . He would come home drunk, and they would fight, and uh, she'd take me to the neighbor, and the police would come and all this. Anyway, that, that

went on for years, . . . I don't know, these ladies just, just didn't believe in leaving these men down there. . . . like until, I think fifth or sixth grade. Because he, uh, things got better for him. Well, I look back on it and I know this because they got better for him because he moved us out of that shack into a brick home.

Evelyn seldom saw her father.

I think the last time I saw him, I was two years old. I don't know where he is. I just, I have a picture of him, that's, that's it. I took it upon myself to look him up one time, and uh, I found him in Fort Worth. And since, he's disappeared on me again.

Evelyn saw her mother regularly on visits during the summer and later when she lived with her, where she saw what she didn't want out of life!

Eve: Sometimes, I would come, um, during the summer because my mother, she was never really stable. . . . I remember visiting her one time in Texas, and then, uh, in Lafayette. She's lived in Lafayette and, she lived in Albany, and now she's living in Hammond. And she's still in her house, near the projects over there. That's where she still lives.

MLL: garbled

Eve: Yah. Because uh, I think, because of, babies, just having babies. I mean she did that. She'd have babies, and she'd have to, and her thing was they, they needed her. She, my mother was on welfare most of her life, raising babies.

So, uh, I definitely had a lot of opportunities to see what I didn't want in my life! (laughing) I mean, it was all around me. I didn't, I did so well. I'd come to visit her, especially the last place over here near the pro-jects, near Daggs-Reid apartment, I mean everybody was pregnant, or either having babies, and I was called a lot of names because I didn't want that! But I just didn't.

When I made fifteen, I came to live with my mother in the projects, and I was in tenth grade at Hammond High. And um, I, like I said, I definitely saw what I didn't want out of my life. So, so I remained on the honor roll. I graduated.

Her graduation was a big family event!

I was the first in four generations to graduate High School. Everybody came! (laughing) My aunts, I mean everybody came. It was, it was a big thing because I was the first one, you know, like I said, in four generations.

Evelyn worked hard to get out of that life and tried college, but didn't succeed. She had worked in food service in high school and college, "the first little black waitress they ever had over there!" When college didn't work out, she enlisted in the Army.

> Eve: After I quit college, I joined the Army. . . . Anyway, um, that's where I found out about my eye disease. In Florida, my basic was in Orlando, Florida. And uh, you know, they check you from head to toe.
>
> My thing, I tried not to leave. I mean when they wanted to discharge me, you know, under honorable, under medical conditions, I tried not to because my thing was, my whole reason for goin was to, well cause I wasn't really smart enough for college, not to make the grades like I was makin in high school. I was embarrassed by C's and D's, I just didn't like that. And uh, so my main reason was to get my mom out of the project. I was gonna just stay in there, I was just going to make a career of it, send the money home, get her out of that neighborhood. So, they found out about my eye disease, and I was, um, medically discharged, honorable discharge under medical conditions, that's how they put it. They kicked me out! That's what they did! (laugh) Anyway, well, well, when you're blind, when you're blind, how, how can do? I mean what can you do?
>
> MLL: Was it just starting?
>
> Eve: The night blindness was getting me. You know you have to pull sentry duty. So the night blindness, that was the first thing to go. In the, in the daytime, I'm, I'm pretty much fine, if I know where I'm goin. Um, they told me then it would take, um, about, they gave me about ten to fifteen years and I would be totally blind.

After this, Evelyn went for training in Job Corp, worked for several years in the medical field as a secretary and in optometry until she was let go when she could no longer read the instruments.

During this time, she married and had two boys. She divorced her husband when "he went to jail," so she has raised the boys alone with no support. Although she lived in her own apartment most of this time, she also spent some time living with her mother, "talk about a pain!" During this time with her mother, she received welfare part of the time and worked part-time in food service.

Then she went for training as a medical transcriptionist in a school for the blind, but since then has not been able to find a job since "the insurance companies will not accept me." She tried babysitting, but no parents left their children since she doesn't have a fenced yard. Since then, she has lived on Social Security disability and food stamps. One

of her brothers occasionally helps the kids with clothes and school materials, but won't give Evelyn anything. She admits to frustration from
all this and says she would like to see a counselor.

When I offered to help her get started doing transcriptions at home
and asked for documentation or references to validate her story, she
said the documents were all at her mother's, and she never produced
them. Her single reference had moved, and Evelyn didn't have her new
phone number. She also clarified that she had not graduated from the
school for the blind since she had missed so many classes attending to
the needs of her sons at school. I suspect that her story is basicly true,
only slightly cleaned up, as most of us tend to do.

Evelyn also had a slight run in with the law because of problems
with the school system, which she shared with me after some hesita-
tion.

> Eve: But now, it's, it's nothin bad. It's just what, when I first moved
> in this neighborhood, the school bus driver didn't want to take my
> sons to school. I mean she, she was like, um, "You've got to have
> this, this particular piece of paper." I'm trying to explain to the lady,
> well from the school, saying that they ride this bus. I'm trying to
> explain to the lady, "I'm legally blind. I can't drive. I can't get out to
> the school. They've already missed two days. Would you please take
> my sons to school?" "No," she had to have the piece of paper! So,
> oh, boy, was I mad! Anyway, um, the judge ended up senten,
> sentencing me to sixty days in jail for losing my temper with the bus
> driver.
> MLL: Oh, wow!
> Eve: I didn't have to spend it, though. I just
> MLL: It was suspended?
> Eve: Ah, yah. No, no, no, I ended up, I spent fifteen days in jail!
> MLL: Oh really!
> Eve: Yes, I did.
> MLL: Oh, wow!
> Eve: Because he was like, "I'm just sick of you people, you know,
> running all," and I'm like he wouldn't even listen to me!

When I asked who she thought the judge meant by "you people,"
Evelyn replied, "Yah, angry, angry black mothers. That's mostly
what's out at that school."

Evelyn's Home
Evelyn's apartment complex was right next to another housing
area that I have visited earlier. Along the road ran a single one-story

building divided into nineteen apartments or condominiums. The building was a greenish-blue color. I drove around the area and saw that there were three buildings total surrounding a quad. The grass and exterior looked very neat. I never saw a person outside, although it was usually hot.

The front door opens into a kitchen about 8 feet by 10 or 12 feet, with kitchen counter on one side, dining table on other side, microwave and a few dishes on the counter. The dining table chairs were white plastic chairs sold for porch furniture. The small kitchen table was dark colored and ragged, definitely well used.

The inside of house was very neat, clean. I could see another room beyond the kitchen with a day bed made up with fluffy, nice covering. The TV was on in the other room and stayed on during the whole time I was there. A window unit air conditioner was in the window next to the door we entered, and it was on.

Evelyn's Explanation for Poverty

Evelyn's explanation for poverty began with her disability, "I'm poor because I'm disabled and can't work!" which continued to rate high in her Card Sorting and Ranking Interview. She had worked hard to try to do better than her mother and made some comments that fit in the Personal Irresponsibility explanation. Evelyn thought a good first impression was important, that it would even overcome a lack of education. But even this has its downside, as one son demonstrated.

> So his grades have dropped, because he says, "Well, momma, they, you know, they, they pick on me. And they'll call me this, and they'll call me that" because I insist that he use proper English. I mean you learn this, you use it! And he said, "They make fun of me, the way I talk."

During her Life History Interview, however, Evelyn began to reflect on the generational problems of poverty.

> Eve: Well, what I have seen, even with my two sisters, it's like a cycle. It's hard to break that welfare thing! Because, you can look from the things that I have told you, it's been hard for me to just not, to just get off of that welfare, and just, just hit that pavement and go do this and go do that, and when one thing didn't work, go try something else. Well, what I've seen, most of 'em don't want to try it. It's easier to just go sit at the welfare office and wait for a check. It's easier to do that than, than to just keep tryin, and keep tryin.

MLL: What are some of the things that make it hard to get off welfare?

Eve: (pause) Well, when I did get off welfare, for the time I had to be on it, uh (pause) it was hard to get a good payin job. I got a minimum wage job. I was working at Wynn Dixie, but that minimum wage job, even in that, it was more than what I was gettin a month on welfare, but then they cut the food stamps. No, no more food stamps, and so see whereas you know, I had two children to feed, there were people that I know that just think that they can't make it without the food stamps. And if they get this job, they will not get any food stamps! And there's a possibility that you won't get the medical card either. You won't git to go to a doctor, neither. And uh, I think, I think that's one of the things that really makes it hard.

MLL: So, the, it's not necessarily the welfare, but it's the things that go along with the welfare, like

Eve: Uhuh, I think that, that would help it a whole lot, say, if they did get this minimum wage job, if they would just get a few food stamps. I mean, maybe not as much as before, but get some food stamps, and at least be able to take their baby to the doctor. Then I don't think it will be, I don't think that they will be as reluctant to give it up.

But then, there are some people, too, that just look as welfare as a way of life. Because their mother was on it, and their mother was on it, and their sisters are on it, and their cousins are on it, everybody's on welfare, you know, and so hey, that's, that's the thing to do! Um, I don't think so! I don't think so!

Yet, Evelyn identified herself as a welfare mother because of the Social Security Disability that she was receiving.

Conclusion

Evelyn was not a simplistic thinker. Her list of the causes of poverty presented in table 12.1 was the most balanced of all the informants. Evelyn pointed out the shortcomings of society: the cycle that keeps new people from entering the job market (can't get a job unless experienced), low pay and lack of benefits, racism in the court system and school system, and insurance companies influencing hiring, but then later reinforced the generational transmission of poverty explanation.

MLL: Well, do you have any other comments? Uh, any questions back here, or other comments about what causes poverty? Or low income?

Eve: I think mine started with my, the people were slaves, and after that sharecroppers. There wasn't much to do for education. We didn't

Table 12.1
Causes of Poverty in General According to Evelyn

Major Causes of Poverty in General
1. Born into poor family
2. Have babies - too many, too early (still in school)
3. Food stamp habit is hard to break
4. Father was absent
5. Too few good jobs
6. Discouraged because past efforts not work well
7. False pride of some black men
8. "No benefits" added to cards: Entry level jobs pay too little and too few hours; many jobs don't have benefits
9. No child support from husband
10. Poverty is a cycle, "can be broken" (added by Evelyn)
11. Teens don't listen to parents to stay in school
12. Mother not helpful (want more money to babysit), not show love
13. Debt
14. Whites don't stay in jail, blacks do, "if Head of Household goes to jail" (E. add)
15. Insurance companies not allow co. to hire you and other disabled
16. Disabled

Minor Causes of Poverty in General
1. Church not help
2. Not have a good presentation, good first impression
3. Mother was single
4. Divorced

Not a Cause of Poverty in General
Husband not work; Uncle drank too much; Aunt did not leave uncle for drinking too much; Raised by aunt and uncle instead of mother; Aunt not work regularly; Have babies—too many, too early (still in school); Not finish college; Not "smart" enough for college; Not apply for jobs because fear discrimination; Quit 7th Ward hospital job, refused job change at Westpark; Not have money to start own business; smoke cigarettes; Brother not help enough; Racism on the job (black man catch hell on white man's job); Parents are content if son is not a druggy or in trouble, so don't push him to get a job; debt; Racism at school, or with school employees; Judges don't listen to poor, ("money's a key factor. More of it you have, easier to get out of jail" added by Eve); Blacks blamed for drugs; Did not save enough money; Need psychological help; There have always been poor people; Discharged by military; Medical card available for welfare people

we didn't have the opportunity for education. And by the time
opportunity came for an education, shoot! I mean so, so many
generations of uneducated people, you can't just throw'em in there
and just say, "Do this." Because, you know, they just, just can't
comprehend it. It's definitely in the genes! It is in the genes! (pause)
MLL: Is it in the genes?
Eve: Hell, yes, I had to study like heck! (laugh) When I went to
college I really had to study! I had to study. Because I was
determined to get out of it. And so, I studied. I didn't, I studied. I
studied well, to make it, to break the cycle. All that work, and I'm
right back in it! That's depressing!

Evelyn's list of causes for poverty in general was the only one that
gave greater weight to ways of thinking than ways of acting, fairly consistent with her answer to question ten of the Causal Differentiation Interview. She was one of the few informants that gave support in the
Card Sorting and Ranking Interview to the Welfare culture explanation
for poverty. Evelyn shared details with many explanations and did not
fit strongly in any.

In reference to her own poverty, as shown in table 12.2, Evelyn's
list continued balanced, but transferred almost all of the responsibility
away from herself to family and society. Only her psychological distress fell into the exclusive individual category of explanations. About
half of the weight fell into the family category, lending her strongest
support to the intergenerational transmission of poverty.

Evelyn on Churches

Evelyn was particularly angry at churches. They trivialized her
problems and thought they understand them.

Eve: When you say what keeps me going, I guess that's it. Not
turning away from God, no matter what. No matter what. She always
told me that, "No matter what you do, always pray. No matter where
you go, find a church. Belong to some congregation." . . .
MLL: Being a part of the church?
Eve: Cause I haven't found a church yet that, and um this pastor, I'm
not goin to mention any names, but I told him about, pretty much
about my life and what I was goin through here, and um, it was like,
well, if I needed a few, a few canned foods or something, well they
had that to give to me. But uh, more or less, there should be a way
that I could live on a little over four hundred dollars a month. I get
four eighty, specifically, a month.

Table 12.2
Causes of Evelyn's Own Low Income

<u>Major Causes for Evelyn's Own Low Income</u>
1. Born into poor family
2. Church not help, "Spiritual help!" (added by Evelyn)
3. Disabled
4. Insurance cor. not allow companies to hire you and other disabled
5. Discharged by military
6. No child support from husband
7. Need psychological help
8. Divorced
9. Poverty is a cycle
10. There have always been poor people
10. Discouraged because past efforts not work well
10. Entry level jobs pay too little and too few hours

<u>Minor Causes of Evelyn's Own Low Income</u>
1. Too few good jobs
2. Many jobs don't have benefits
3. Mother not helpful (want more money to babysit) and not show love
4. Medical card available for welfare people
5. Mother was single, "being born into a single parent family"
6. Father was absent
7. Food stamp habit is hard to break
8. Did not save money, "Wasn't taught to save money, taught to pay bills, get what you need to live, tomorrow not promised" (added by Evelyn)

<u>Not a Cause of Evelyn's Own Low Income</u>
False pride of some black men; Husband not work; Uncle drank too much; Aunt did not leave uncle for drinking too much; Raised by aunt and uncle instead of mother; Aunt not work regularly; Have babies—too many, too early (still in school); Not finish college; Not "smart" enough for college; Not apply for jobs because fear discrimination; Quit 7th Ward hospital job, refused job change at Westpark; Not have money to start own business; smoke cigarettes; Brother not help enough; Racism on the job (black man catch hell on white man's job); Parents are content if son is not a druggy or in trouble, so don't push him to get a job; debt; Racism at school, or with school employees; Judges don't listen to poor; Blacks blames for drugs; Whites don't stay in jail, black do; Not have a good presentation, good first impression; Teens don't listen to parents to stay in school

Evelyn also picked up the selective Bible reading in churches that may lead to hypocrisy.

And it took everything to move here. You know, the transfer of the lights and the moving, and everything. And I didn't have groceries. They brought me groceries, and uh, encouraged me to come to church. And prayed with me, and for me. And um, encouraged me that, to, to ask, if I needed something, to ask, because they knew my situation.

And once I started asking, then, well, you know, I felt like I was gettin on their nerves! You know, so I don't ask anymore! I, I just don't! I just say, "Well, Lord, it's up to you because well, I mean, I've got to have some pride!"

I mean like if, I think that my church can send thousands of dollars to Mexico every month, or two thousand dollars here, two thousand dollars over there, why can't we spend a couple of those thousand, and take care of our people in our own church? You know, because it you've ever been on a fixed income, that doesn't last a whole month! You know, and so there are people right here in our congregation at the end of the month, they just don't have. But you know, they'd rather send it someplace else. Instead of, you know, give to the people right there. So needless to say, I don't go to church over there very much. I need to find a home church. I really do! Try to have a chat (church?).

There's this other church that my mom went to. I won't mention any names there either, but she still goes to this church. Oh, they believe in tithe, pay your tithe, pay your tithe. (laugh) But uh, at the same time, the preacher has been known to say quote, unquote, "This, the church is not on welfare," meaning, you know, "We don't have anything to give." Well now, my Bible says that the church ought to be run on tithe and offering. Am I right? You know, and if widows and orphans are to be taken care of by that! OK, well, I don't know. I haven't found a church that believes that yet! So, so I keep smilin and I keep prayin and I keep talkin to the Lord!

CHAPTER 13
MARY'S STORY

Mary was a woman about five feet tall with salt and pepper hair that was normally pulled back. She looked to be in her forties. She also had several growths or warts on her face. Mary usually dressed casually, for example, a white pull over shirt with horizontal colored stripes and white pants with virtical blue stripes.

Mary's definition of herself was "mother." Her son and daughter were the most important things in her life! Her daughter was already in college on an art scholarship. Her son was in junior high and giving her fits. When I first visited her, here is what occurred.

> I asked Mary, "How are you doing?" She replied something like, "I've been sick for five weeks, and I just put my son in the Berean Home." (The Berean Home is a temporary home for runaways and troubled youth.) I lamented, and she continued with a discussion of which I remember the following, "Since December, I had kidney problems and bleeding ulcers." I asked how old her son is, and she said he is thirteen. She said when she gets upset about her son, she vomits blood.

Mary thought her Catholic upbringing was a big influence on her life. "We grew up extremely Catholic." According to her, she was raised to be a mother and housewife, not to support a family.

> I was strictly born, as far as my parents were concerned, to get married and have children and raise children. My father helped send my brothers to college. Sent them to private high schools. Taught them to drive. We were women, we got none of that!

She was born and raised in New Orleans in a middle class family, where she and her siblings went to Catholic schools. Her father was a pharmacist. She says her life was sheltered, even with somewhat harsh parenting. This stable upbringing came to an abrupt end in high school.

> Pregnant at seventeen, and my dad had about two months before that had a heart attack, so I was kicked out of my parents' house. And it went down hill from there! (laugh) . . . Yep, so it was once again one of those times I had to deal with it myself cause my parents had nothing to do with me at that time, being, you know, little staunch Catholics that they were. So, I'm not real sure I ever recovered totally from it.

She gave up the baby, went to college for a few years and soon married another man. Two children were born, and she stayed home, but later they were able to work. "And he was making around forty-five thousand. . . . I averaged thirty thousand a year."

After a decade of marriage, Mary's husband suddenly left her for another woman!

> When he left, he took all my jewelry, he burned all my clothes, he emptied out our account, he took our car. I mean literally, and left me with three months of bills. He had kept me away from the house. So, the hole was real deep! Ladder was real shaky!

To her anger, when Mary received her divorce, she recieved no help from family or church, but was shuttled onto the welfare line.

> So, literally as I told you before, the courts set it up that I would go on welfare! And it was literally put that way! This was recently done on another case, too. The mother was working recently, and Judge xxx told her to quit and stay home with the children!

I think that what angered Mary was not that she had to receive welfare in order to stay at home with her children, which she did for four years and said she did not regret that because they needed her since her ex-husband had abandoned them, but that the court set a low child support so she would qualify for welfare! Then they shuttled the dazed woman off to welfare out of their way! She survived off of child support and welfare of about $350 per month and food stamps of $300 for four years.

And it was nothing but survival! There were days I would feed them, and I would not eat! And the only one who really saw it was my daughter, and she knew what was going on. Now no matter what people say about the welfare system, (pause) no matter what, you know, the amount you give now and have been given for the past years, it's not even an existence! You know, it's horrendous!

Despite the fact that welfare was cut when she began, Mary went back to school for three years to finish her degree in marketing supported by grants, loans and scholarships. "They told me literally that if I would quit school, they would give me my benefits back the next day." That didn't resolve their problems. Mary has worked now for over three years, but there's still little income. Her income from work last year was $7000.

Mary: And I'm, by no means, out of the hole! I earn, right now, seven an hour. (pause) I tend, until I got sick, I was working right at fifty hours a week. Child support is supposed to be three hundred and forty a month, and he sends it when he wants to! So basically, we're living on the seven. (pause)
MLL: And you did mention that they do, the company does have good benefits.
Mary: Oh, we have great insurance! Um, I actually have a savings account with the company. Um,
MLL: Retirement?
Mary: Uhum, well, I have a 401K. I mean I have all of about three hundred dollars ($300) in it.
MLL: Right.
Mary: But they still match it. They match sixteen percent, which is pretty high for a company! It is an international company now. So, just the medical insurance, and both of the young kids need braces. And there's a set amount they'll give for braces which is about three quarters the amount, you know, the total amount. (Pause) Mostly I pay off student loans. I seem to buy a great deal of shoes!

And the pain is not just financial. Mary suffers because her children have suffered through a divorce and poverty. "But the biggest thing was that I had seen how hurt my children are, especially my oldest one by her dad's choices." And Mary suffers with the burden of raising the children alone.

I think my heaviest burden has been the decisions. I have never been strong, have a strong enough ego in being a mother to ever feel like I was making the right decisions.

In fact, we figured this out one day, it's eleven years in August, I've been by myself, and I have had a total of two and a half weeks, seventeen days, of not having twenty-four hour whatever of the kids. Never got a break! You know, husband gives you break now and then, that's not what I mean. He's, he's never taken them. My family has never taken them. The most he ever takes them is a couple of days to New Orleans, or he's taken them to Alabama, but that's never been more than four days.

Between the decisions and never having a break, I think that's what has gotten me to the point physically that I am. And you know, once this, it has taken ten years in this whole problem, it will easily take me twenty to get out of it.

According to Mary, this ego was first hurt by the harsh treatment at home, then the "brainwashing" she received at the home for unwed mothers and then by the divorce and how her family and church reacted to it.

According to the pastor, I was white trash! I begged xxx private school to take my children on scholarship. Both of them had read since three years old! Both of, I mean, I have spent time with them. I mean that's the difference. And the school would do nothing! I mean I offered to be janitor to pay for it! I offered to do anything to get what I consider a better education! No way!

Added to that was the indignity of receiving welfare.

MLL: By the hole, do you mean debts, or do you just mean the, the income that you have now? What do you mean by hole?
Mary: (pause) It's a mentality. You know, I can remember walking in for welfare, and we're talking now ten years, so statistics have very much changed. I felt like such a low life! That I didn't belong there! I mean, I know that I am an intelligent person. What in the hell am I doing in the welfare office? And I sit there, and it would be like I have no choice because my kids. And it builds, when you already have a low ego, and this is what you have to sit through! And then they tell you how wrong you are for doing what you're doing, as far as going to school and not staying on welfare. It's, it's more, it's a combination. It's the mentality. They are giving you this! Think about how people think of this! I paid taxes for years! I know I did not receive it from welfare, the amounts I paid in taxes! But I was still made to feel this was given to me because I was trash! And you, that stays with you!

Mary's Home

Mary lived in a duplex in neighborhood of about thirty to forty homes which she had received help to buy. The duplex was nice, but the surrounding neighborhood was ragged and dark. The duplexes are built of blond or sand colored brick, with gray shingles. The roads are concrete, with sidewalks.

There were few cars in the area. There was trash on the street. The grass looked like it had been mowed very recently, although there were no grass cuttings on the sidewalks. There was an eighteen inch wide flower bed which ran in front of the porch which had blooming pansies in it. There were two metal chairs and a hanging plant on the porch.

The front door opens to the living room that had nice matching overstuffed sofa and chair, light blue print with wood trim, which sits very low. Besides the sofa and chair, there is a five foot tall, twenty-four inch bookshelf, an entertainment center with a twenty-seven inch TV, a pressed board desk of the type sold in Walmart and another small TV. The floor is tile, but there is a nondescript rug spead in front of and slightly under the edge of the couch. The tile floor is sprinkled with small pieces of paper, dust, things sitting on floor.

The kitchen is in front of the front door, with a wall blocking part of the view and next to it is the dining room in the far right hand corner. The kitchen counter is a pleasing dark green, with oak wood doors. The dining room table and chairs are a matched wood set of probably moderate cost. It looks to be two inch thick wood, not pressed board.

Mary's Explanation for Poverty

When first told about the purpose of this research, Mary immediately responded, "It's because I'm divorced." Later, the interview concluded with this exchange.

> Mary: It's the courts! When I got divorced, Judge xxx literally gave me a divorce and enrolled me in welfare at the same time! In Louisiana, they're great about giving custody of the children to the mother, but not . . .
> MLL: the money.
> Mary: And it was, was literally said by my attorney, "We're giving you this amount cause this will put you on welfare, and you'll get food stamps and the medical card."

During her Card Sorting Interview, however, Mary put "where God wants the person" as the primary cause of poverty, both in general and in her case, seen in tables 13.1 and 13.2. She clarified that she didn't think that poverty was some kind of punishment from God, but she was simply recognizing God's sovereignty in her and others' lives.

After God's will, Mary returned to divorce and its consequences as the major causes of poverty, both in general and in her case. She definitely blamed the husbands for leaving their ex-wives and children in poverty, but also, as a divorced mother, accepted responsibility for the decisions the mother makes after the divorce, the decision to leave the children and work to support the family or to go on welfare to care for the children.

Table 13.1
Causes of Poverty in General According to Mary

Major Causes of Poverty in General
1. Where the Lord wants the person
2. Divorce, Husband leave wife in debt
3. Choice
4. Girls raised to be housewives only, Lack education to make money, Lack of education
5. Employers discriminate against: single mothers, age, gender, poverty level applicants; Low salary
6. Single motherhood, Courts set up single mother for welfare, Little or irregular child support
7. Finish college late
8. Mother not work outside in order to care for children

Minor Causes of Poverty in General
1. The thinking imposed by welfare, Welfare stops when begin college
2. Lack of confidence in self, Way of thinking about self, No help from family
3. Sickness, School loans, Credit cards
4. Kicked out of parents' home, Pregnant at early age, Thinking imposed at home for unwed mothers

Not a Cause of Poverty in General
Society's need to feel superior; Social service organizations treat poor as receivers only; society's need to blame someone, born into poor family; refusing to accept possibility of divorce; the welfare system; the Catholic Church's rigid doctrines, impose guilt; abusive husband; abusive parents; lack of dignity for welfare recipients; kids wanting name brands, other things

It seemed that Mary's anger came from three sources. First, she felt inadequate to make these kind of choices (to care for children or to sup-port family) and resented being forced to do so. Second, she was angry at her ex-husband and others who don't provide adequately for the children after the divorce. Third, she was angry at the state for their role in this. It began with being pushed into welfare by an "impartial" judge and her own lawyer. It continued with being made to feel like trash and having her children's child support confiscated by the state. (According to Mary, when the mother receives welfare in Louisiana, the state confiscates all of the child support paid above $50 per month.) And continued through being criticized by caseworkers for daring to go to college.

Table 13.2
Causes of Mary's Own Low Income

Major Causes of Mary's Own Low Income
1. Where the Lord wants the person
2. Choice, Mother not work outside in order to care for children, Single motherhood
3. Husband leave wife in debt, Little or irregular child support, Divorce, Way of thinking about self, Lack of confidence in self, Abusive husband
4. Courts set up single mother for welfare, Lack education, Lack of education to make money
5. Employers discriminate against: single mothers, age, gender, poverty level applicants; Low salary

Minor Causes of Mary's Own Low Income
1. School loans, Finish college late
2. Girls raised to be housewives only

Not a Cause of Mary's Own Low Income
Society's need to feel superior; Social service organizations treat poor as receivers only; society's need to blame someone, born into poor family; refusing to accept possibility of divorce; the welfare system; the Catholic Church's rigid doctrines, impose guilt; abusive parents; lack of dignity for welfare recipients; kids wanting name brands, other things; no help from family; credit cards; sickness; welfare stops when begin college; the thinking imposed by welfare; thinking imposed at home for unwed mothers; kicked out of parent's home; pregnant at early age

A final matter was the discrimination against single mothers. Mary reported that employers were reluctant to hire single mothers because of the possible interference with their job by the children's needs.

Conclusion

While Mary was angry principally at her ex-husband and the court system for their injustice, she still saw her own role in her low income through the choices she made trying to cope with injustice. Mary was about the only informant to support the ethos argument through the religious and cultural barbs she threw at xxx Church. Her explanation for poverty was heavily weighted toward acting causes, but within that area, it was very balanced perceptions between social and individual causes. Her explanation for poverty does not fit within any of the ten explanations from the literture review.

CHAPTER 14
OLIVIA'S STORY

Olivia is a white woman in her early twenties. She was nice looking, with light makeup, light colored hair pulled neatly back in a ponytail, slightly emaciated figure. She usually wore shorts and a blouse. Olivia was born in New Orleans. When she was five, her mother divorced and remarried and moved to California. Her step dad worked as a pharmacist, and her mother opened her own daycare. She didn't get along with either of them.

Olivia: Problems at home really messed me up with my schoolwork. So then I didn't end up finishing school at all. . . . Well, I uh, so I left home at seventeen. . . . my relationship with my mom. Ne, we never were close. We never could talk. We never did anything for each other. We didn't enjoy each other at all. We just hated each other! So there was, there was no real emotional support and that kind of thing going on.

MLL: And your step dad

Olivia: No, I didn't get along with him at all. He thought little girls should be seen and not heard, and we didn't get along. We didn't talk. (laugh) We didn't do anything! Just like, me and my mom. In fact he, he tried ta (pause).

Remember one time he was mad at me, and jumped on me, knocked me to the ground. But I (laugh), but I hit him hard. I actually hit him hard enough that he went away. That was cool. And I'll tell you what, and uh, my mother heard a thump when he knocked me to the ground. And he's literally like on me, with his knees on my torso. She heard a thump and by, by, and so she came out of her bedroom at few minutes later, by the time we were already up and he was back sittin on his sofa. And I was really upset. I said, "He just jumped on me!" She didn't believe me. Called me a liar.

Beginning at age thirteen Olivia often slept outdoors, "I would be out of the house for like a week, sleeping in the grass at a park or something!" Her dad in New Orleans "did nothing to help me! Nothing!" She eventually married at age seventeen. They moved to Kansas and had two children. But her husband was irritated by the noise of the babies.

> Olivia: When I had my first child, he would not hold him, touch him, change his diaper, act at all like he cared that this kid was around! In fact, the kid was a bother! If the kid would cry, when he's trying to watch TV or whatever, and it's botherin him, and we lived in a trailer, a travel trailer, the child and I would have to go outside! This was in Kansas in the winter.
> MLL: Um, pretty cold.
> Olivia: And so, that was all a very miserable experience, and he just didn't care at all. It was him! If the baby was cryin, no, let the baby cry while I fix him a sandwich! Grown man! Well, that was miserable, too, so actually by the time I was pregnant, by the time the second one was born, while I was pregnant with the first one [sic], I left him because I just wasn't raising kids like that, you know.

Her husband had encouraged Olivia to get her GED, so when she left him, she moved in with relatives in Texas and went to school to become a nurse. She got school loans to help with costs and became a registered nurse. Then,

> The week in between finals and graduation, that last year, I moved out during that week into a little rent house. Me and my two little kids. And just been workin fulltime in nursing for years and raisin two children.

Olivia eventually bought the rent house, and life looked good. Then the stress of her job began to get to her.

> I love nursing. I love taking care of patients. I took care of very, very, in my favorite job, I took care of some very, very, very ill patients on, on the medicine floor, which has like TB, AIDS, cancer, uh the alcoholics, GI bleeders, all this kind of stuff. And uh, that's all very interesting to me. I love to, I love to both learn about the illnesses and the treatments, and I also love to take care of that patient, make that patient comfortable, you know, whatever, answer his questions so he's not scared, or frame'em, whatever. I love to take care of the patient, make him feel good, comfortable. . . . This was my favorite job that I was just tellin you, they were short staffed,

and they had very, very sick patients! And I mean, you would have so many of them that you had to be on your toes. (snap fingers three times) We never sat down! And we never had a minute to relax. And uh, I was scared, but, first of all, I was totally stressed out! And hollering at my kids every day, to get away, away from me, when I'd get home. But I was also scared I might miss something! And you don't want patients to die just because you miss something!

Perhaps she was a little over responsible, but this led to a severe depression.

Near the end of ninety-four, I just became so depressed. I, have major depression, which is an illness. . . . I had a couple of bad bouts that maybe lasted a few weeks or months, and uh, over the years. And kind of a continuous steady depression.

I was like always withdrawn. I didn't have any friends. I didn't want to talk to anyone. I didn't want to go out. I didn't wanta, you know, and uh, I don't know, a couple of the other symptoms.

So, anyway, in the end of ninety-four, I just got one so bad! And I kept thinking it would go away, and it just did not go away. It just, and it was so bad! It was horrible! (pause) Before I quit my job, I was taking my lunch breaks and going laying in the back seat of my car, curled up in a ball, and I would drag myself out after lunch time and, uh, which I usually took an hour instead of the allotted half an hour, I would drag myself out of my car and go upstairs and just kinda space out. You know, I just wasn't doin much of anything. I couldn't concentrate, I couldn't do anything.

And uh, finally, one day, you just cannot even get up. Finally one day, the bell rings, and its' time to get up to get ready for work, and you're just not doin it. And so, I just laid there, in the bed, like the whole day, like talkin to no one, not doing anything, not, nothing. And that's what I did for like the next, about the next two years.

For two years, Olivia only got up to get money from her credit cards to live off of and pay bills by mail. "I would barely drink a glass of water a day cause I didn't want to get up and go to the bathroom." Her relatives, but not her mother, dad or step dad, tried to help.

My family came around a couple of times to tell me what to do, to insult me, to threaten me, to pass judgment on me, and mixed in with that, I know nobody's perfect, mixed in with that, if there was some understanding, some support, anything of that nature, I would have been alright with it, I guess. But there was none of that! It was only "let's go to Olivia's and insult her, and threaten her and tell her what to do!" It just hurt me so bad! And it was just useless! They just had nothing, they say they want to help, and I guess they do want to help, but I'm tellin them, "what you're doin's not helpin, whatta doin's making it worse, whatta doin is hurtin me," and they're just not listening. And they just keep doin it. So I finally had to cut them off. I cut them off after like a year. Because I don't need that! The last thing I need is people saying they love me and then throwin around insults when I'm in the depths of depression. I just don't!

Towards the end of the two years, Olivia realized that this couldn't go on and began working at an agency as a replacement nurse. She filed for bankruptcy. Her house was repossessed by the bank after trying to sell it for a year. She became suicidal.

Olivia: So I had been very suicidal, and uh, I had been tryin to kill myself! I had so many ways to do it. Places I could do it, cause I didn't want to do it at home cause then my children would find me, and I didn't want that. Poor kids, how, you know, that would have been (pause) horrible.

And uh, (pause) I just couldn't do it! I just kept tryin to do it, and I just couldn't do the last thing I had to do to do it. I could have everything all ready, and all I have to do, you know, it whatever this one thing, and I couldn't do it. And I was tryin.

MLL: I'm glad!

Olivia: I was tryin to make, thank you. I haven't decided if I am or not, yet. (laugh) Cause it's been a rough road. But, so after tryin, kept sort of like reasoning with myself, "Just do it! Just go ahead!" And it, I mean, it's just torture! It's torture! I'm so miserable! I can't even make myself kill myself! And that's when I went for help, cause I was, it was just redic. . ., God, it was horrible, and stupid, and I said, "Well, I haven't gone back for help."

This began Olivia's battles with the community. The community health clinic wouldn't help her unless she was admitted as a patient, which she wouldn't do because of her kids. Her doctor gave her some medicine, but it was too expensive to buy. Finally she went to the emergency room, threatened suicide and was admitted as an outpatient.

Churches ignored her. Social service organizations refused her. Olivia applied for disability, but it was delayed for years without an answer. She sued for welfare and won after a year's battle.

Olivia: Um, I tried signing up for welfare shortly after I had decided not to use the credit cards anymore. (laugh) I went over there, and uh, tried to sign up. The welfare office took a year! Well, they gave me food stamps right away. So I've been on food stamps since then, but they took a year to finally give me AFDC and Medicaid. I went there and applied a hundred million times, and uh, they just wouldn't give it to me. I'd say, "I've got two kids. I can't work. There's no money." "Nope. Sorry, can't help ya." "I need this medications. If I had these medications, I might get well! You know, and I might be able to get back to work." "Nope, sorry, can't help ya." So, and so I finally got a lawyer.

MLL: What reason did they give?

Olivia: Oh, God! "Your car is worth too much money," which it wasn't, by far. It was hundreds under the allowed amount. "You're not telling the truth," was a nice one. It's hard, it was hard, they didn't believe I was telling the truth any of the times I went, I don't think. People lie so much, I guess. . . . They've become very callous. They don't care very much. Um, (pause) those are the main things.

MLL: Hum. I didn't realize that could happen.

Olivia: And the man, the man, one of the workers who was in the hearing, one of the workers who was my worker at that time, lied! Lied! He was saying it was my fault because they told me to do something and I never did it, when they, the fact is, they never told me to do that, whatever it was. And he lied to that judge and said that, so he lied under oath to try to make it my fault and to try to keep me off welfare! I'm in major depression! I've got two kids, you know, that I am the sole support, and the man is lying to keep me off welfare! The, the, the man in the welfare office! (tapping on the table) Oh, my hair is, you know how when you get upset and your hair feels tinglely in the back? It's doin that. Oh, mad, mad, mad, mad.

MLL: Hum.

Olivia: I had welfare about two days after that. No, it was the next morning.

Despite the welfare, Olivia was homeless at the time of the interviews, so she left her children with the relatives who had kept her while going to school and headed to Hammond to look for a job.

I met Olivia through contact with a local social service organization. She had found a job cleaning offices twice a week and was living in her car. She slept in a tent she set up a local campgrounds, the fourth so far. She couldn't find an apartment that she could accumulate enough money to pay the deposit.

Olivia's Home

Olivia's home was her small red, late model coupe. It was filled to the brim with clothes, sleeping bags and camping equipment. The front seat and floor space was reserved for papers, bills and other important items. When I mentioned her tent as her home, she emphasized that her car was her home.

Her tent was a small round, half a soccer ball shaped tent. It looked too small to sleep stretched out and perhaps she curled up to sleep. The tent was set up in a local campground. An employee there invited Olivia to stay with her for a few days, and perhaps she found a new home.

Olivia's Explanation for Poverty

Olivia immediately and repeatedly identified the cause of her poverty to be her depression, an illness. Before she became severely depressed, she felt that she was living well, in her own house, raising her children.

Once she became depressed and was reduced to poverty, she also became very angry that her family and community did nothing to help, in her opinion.

> Olivia: I have been in Texas for all these years with my family (pause) insulting me and calling that help. With every, I even called the churches in town. I've been to just everything, anything and everything I could find, anywhere, to help me and have been refused by all of them! The only one that didn't refuse me was the one people who paid that electric bill. Refused by all of them. I, I applied for the low-income apartments, which by the way, cost me twenty dollars ($20) to apply. . . . And uh, so she refused.
>
> MLL: After you paid.
>
> Olivia: . . . I went to the mayor and said, "Look, this woman's not letting me in her house, housing apartments." He called her up (laugh). The mayor called her up when I was sitting in her office. Told her to let me in, you know. (pause,) Pss (blow air out) She didn't let me in. She refused me because my credit. . . .
>
> MLL: Didn't make any difference.
>
> Olivia: So I mean there was no emergency housing. They wouldn't even let me on the list for section eight in the projects! They, they said they're not even taking applications. And I asked them several times. They wouldn't let me in the low-income housing. And just, not, nobody, nowhere, I just got refused. I mean I couldn't even think right now how many times I was refused. And for what stupid reasons, but they all had reasons, and I was refused everywhere. And so, what happened was "I don't wanta be in Texas anymore!" (Laugh) . . .
>
> People in Texas, maybe it's just me or whatever, they're so judgmental that I just can't stand it! And, and it guess it's all part of this gettin refused all the time thing. You know, they, they say

they're here to help, and they say they're gonna help, and they say they love their brothers and mankind and all this bullshit, and you go for some damned help cause you're in serious need, "Nope. Sorry, can't help you."

This anger with the community was reflected in the responses in Olivia's Card Sorting Interview, shown in Table 14.1.

Table 14.1
Causes of Poverty in General According to Olivia

Major Causes of Poverty in General
1. Whole community not accept responsibility to help poor
2. Welfare: not train for job, deduct salary from check, cut off medical [if lose job], cut off if receive $1000 loan for college, Welfare delayed: worker lie, late medical card
3. Minimum wage is too low
4. Few good jobs available
5. Prejudice versus: blacks, homeless, poor dressers
6. Ex-husband: not caring, not send child support

Minor Causes of Poverty in General
1. Born into poor family / environment raised in
2. Unhealthy family workings (title given by Olivia); Mom like sister more; Little contact with Dad, no help given; Not get along with mom; Step dad wants girls to be quiet, aggressive, alcoholic; Left home early"
3. Individual not accept responsibility for actions
4. Community refusing to help (title given by Olivia): Mental health clinic not help, Low income apartment: refused, lie about application, Lawyer irresponsible, Community not help, SSI refused, Churches not help, Others judge, hate poor
5. Was divorced / is single mother
6. Working part-time
7. Mental Illness (title given by Olivia): Major depression, People don't understand depression, Family not understand depression
8. Not understand and knowledge how money and interest works, how to make money with money

Not a Cause of Poverty in General
High taxes on middle class, Not social, not have friends, Work as a nurse: work all shifts, stress, understaffed, requires clear thinking, House not sell, Home schooling, Rich people get free services / poor people pay, Banks are dishonest, No mentors, No union for nurses, Credit cards, Difficulty finding good babysitters, Student loans for college, Get GED instead of high school diploma, Parents divorced

The first five major causes were all directed right at the community. She was angry that others did not understand depression.

> People who, because people don't seem to believe in, particularly depression, it's not the depression everybody gets, it's an illness. It's a different thing, and it's very, very bad. People tend to sorta take the attitude, "There's nothing wrong with you. Get a job and stop whining. . . ." I mean please open your eyeballs, America, and see that it's not! I would not, you know, a normal person would not just decide, "Well, I'm just not going to work. I'm going to get on welfare." And then sit around to the point that they've lost everything. See what I mean, does that make sense?

Olivia also didn't understand the logic of dropping the amount of welfare a person receives for every bit the person earns.

> I think ninety-nine percent (99%) of people in this country, if you could make the same exact amount of money, settin around doin nothin as you could goin off to work, you'd set around an do nuthin! I mean, really!

And, according to Olivia, welfare discouraged people from getting education and improving themselves because it is cut off if the recipient starts college.

> Olivia: When you, if you try to go to college and you get a student loan, if you get over a thousand dollars, they'll cut you off welfare. . . Yes, sir! So that, uh, you know, if you do decide to go to college, again you want to improve yourself, you're tired of livin like this, and you want to go to college, well, you're gonna get cut off welfare! So that you can't afford to go to college, even with a loan, because now you have no welfare. Now you have no money to help you feed your children. Now you have no money to pay your rent. Now you have no money to live on while you're in college. So instead of encouraging people to go to college, they
> MLL: discourage
> Olivia: yah, they make it hard on them.

And churches, well, "Churches, I love the churches! Psuh (blows air out of mouth)," she exclaimed with sarcasm.

Generally, only secondary causes in Olivia's Card Sorting and Ranking Interview came from individual or familial sources. During the Causal Differentiation Interview, Olivia mentioned that growing up in a welfare family could shape the children's expectations for life.

Table 14.2
Causes of Olivia's Own Low Income

Major Causes of Olivia's Own Low Income
1. Major depression
2. Family not understand depression, or care to help
3. Whole community not accept responsibility to help poor, Texas not help, SSI refused, Churches not help, Welfare delayed: worker lie, late medical card, People don't understand depression
4. Not social, not have friends
5. Was divorced / is single mother
6. Ex-husband: not caring, not send child support

Minor Causes for Olivia's Own Low Income
1. Bad home life (title given by Olivia): Not get along with mom, Parents divorced, Step dad wants girls to be quiet, aggressive, alcoholic, Left home early, Little contact with dad, no help given
2. Work as a nurse: work all shifts, stress, understaffed, requires clear thinking,
3. Prejudice versus: blacks, homeless, poor dressers
4. Minimum wage is too low
5. Low income apartment: refused, lie about application

Not a Cause for Olivia's Own Low Income
Mental health clinic delayed, Mom like sister more, Other judge, hate poor, Individual not accept responsibility for actions, High taxes on middle class, Not understand how money and interest works, Born into poor family / environment raised in, Welfare: not train for job, deduct salary from check, cut off medical [if job}, cut off is if receive $1000 loan for college, Working part-time, Few good jobs available, House not sell, Home schooling, Rich people get free services / poor people pay, Banks are dishonest, No mentors, No union for nurses, Lawyer irresponsible, Credit cards, Difficulty finding good babysitters, Student loans for college, Get GED instead of high school diploma

"It's kinda the environment you were raised in." But Olivia didn't want to think about her mother and upbringing and how that might influence her situation.

Olivia: I didn't know we were going to talk about my mom.
MLL: Oh, OK. Well, we were talking about you, we, we don't have to, we can stop, if you want. It's just that, uh, you know, I'm interested in things that had an influence on where you're at today,

and that, that can make a difference. Help, you don't have to say anything you don't want to.
Olivia: I don't like to think about her. I'm still really angry with her. I think she was a horrible mother. Huh (blows air out), makes me sick, even still as I think back. Just makes me sick.
MLL: OK.
Olivia: It's no excuse. I mean I know that kids were abused worse than I was. I think I was emotionally abused. You know. But I mean, the kids, the kids that were abused worse than I was, their mothers make me sick, too! You know? I mean, it's just disgusting! It's just gross!

In reference to her own low income shown in Table 14.2, Olivia did switch much of the cause for poverty away from the community to scattered individual reasons: depression, extended family that did not understand and help, lack of support from nonexistent friends and a very real ex-husband.

Olivia did have a suggestion for a solution to the problem of poverty.

MLL: Number nine: when someone is poor, whose fault is it?
Olivia: Oh, get a grip! What do you mean, whose fault is it? Nobody's fault! (pause) I really think instead of being split, (sigh) I really think people should come together more. But I know it's not realistic, and it's not gonna happen. . . . The really, really rich, are so overflowing with money that they don't know what to do with, they don't care. But it's the middle class who works their butt off, but if, I mean, if they would stop and take a good look at any one of these people, they would probably find a human, you know, with regular human problems. And maybe, they could help. Whose, OK, when someone is poor, whose fault is it? (pause) It's nobody's fault. It's just the way things are. Uh, is it my fault if my daddy was president? Is it my fault if my daddy is some rich billionaire, owner of something, uh, Gates, what's his name? Is it my fault if my daddy lives in government housing and sells drugs? That's not the per, the person's fault, where they are is where they are.

Think it's a question of gettin them out of where they are. And if you want to know who, whose responsibility it is to get them out of where they are, it's their responsibility and all of us as a community responsibility. That's whose responsibility it is. Everybody responsibility. We're all here together. (pause)

You know, if you want to lower crime, start workin with the poor people in your city, you know. If you want to improve your property value, start working with the poor people in your city. (pause)

You can't totally solve the problem. Some people are gonna be what they're gonna be, you know. But most people don't like living in roach infested, falling down houses. Most people don't like havin to scratch and, for meals. Most people don't like havin to walk everywhere, or bum rides off of people because they can't afford a car. You know, most people if you offer them a chance, they're gonna take it. Not everybody, just most of'em.

Conclusion
In reference to poverty in general, Olivia gave a very high weight to structural causes (71%), but it doesn't really fit the U.S. Structural Problems or Structural Sin explanations since it is very community oriented. It is very highly acting weighted (90%). In reference to her own low income, Olivia gave a balanced view between thinking and acting and between individual and social causes. No individual explanation from the literature search is strongly supported.

CHAPTER 15
CONCLUSIONS ABOUT INFORMANTS'
EXPLANATIONS FOR POVERTY

The informants above had diverse backgrounds, life-stories, ethnicity, work history, living conditions and explanations for poverty. What they often had in common were the anger or pain caused by poverty. Learning with them was an emotional growth experience for me that fundamentally changed the way I view poor people.

Support of Experts' Explanations

On a more analytical note, as each informant's explanation for poverty was presented, it was compared with the ten explanations for poverty from the literature review. The only explanation for poverty from the literature review that was supported by every informant was the U.S. Structural Problems explanation. It also received the highest aver-age weight.[1] Also on the social side of the scale, the Welfare Culture explanation only received scattered support, and Ethos explanation was supported only by one informant.

On the individual side of the scale, Personal Irresponsibility was acknowledged by two thirds of the informants as a significant cause of poverty. The family was recognized by about half of the informants to have influence on income through the Culture of Poverty, Human Resources and Material Culture explanations.

---

[1] Each reason listed in their Card Sort and Stacking exercise was assigned a number in descending order and then assigned to fit with certain explanations by the experts. These "weights" refer to the numerical total of each category on the grid after each informant's answers were distributed.

Although in the Causal Differentiation Interview, two thirds of the informants gave priority to ways of thinking as a cause of poverty, in the Card Sorting and Ranking Interview, eight of the nine informants gave strong priority to ways of acting as a cause of poverty. Only one informant gave approximately equal weight to both ways of acting and ways of thinking.

Thinking / Acting Continuum

As seen in Tables 15.1 and 15.2, the informants displayed a strong preference for ways of acting (76%) causing poverty more than ways of thinking (25%). This contradicted the answers of the majority of the in-formants to question ten of the Causal Differentiation Interview, where two-thirds gave preference to ways of thinking as being the cause of poverty. This is probably explained by the popular acceptance among North Americans of the axiom of "thinking determining behavior" as taught by Weber's theories of ideology, and more impor-tantly, through pop psychology based on Freud and others.

Table 15.1
Average of Grids of Explanations for Poverty in General
According to Race and Income Source (Welfare or Working)

Category of Informant	Average Value		
	Individual	Social	
Black, Welfare	43%	58%	
Black, Working	63%	38%	
White, Welfare	33%	67%	
White, Working	55%	45%	
	"We"	"He"	"They"
Black, Welfare	30%	13%	58%
Black, Working	52%	11%	38%
White, Welfare	17%	16%	67%
White, Working	39%	16%	45%
	Thinking	Acting	
Black, Welfare	24%	76%	
Black, Working	23%	77%	
White, Welfare	12%	88%	
White, Working	38%	62%	

Note: Values may not add up to 100% due to rounding. None can be "generalized" to general public.

Importance of Education

This emphasis on ways of acting causing poverty, if supported by a quantitative study, may have significance to the importance of education in most plans to fight poverty. In the grid Figure 8.1 earlier, education is found in three different spots. The Culture of Poverty and Human Resources explanations include the training and education of children by their parents. The two structural explanations and the Welfare Culture explanation include the training provided to students by the educational system.

These informants would emphasize, however, not what one knows, but how one acts and is acted upon by others and by society as the greater causes of poverty. Only three of the nine informants, all black, thought a lack of education or a poor education was a major cause of poverty in the Card Sorting and Ranking Interview.

In general, the less educated informants indicated their educational deficiency as a cause of poverty, while the better educated informants turned to other reasons, both in reference to themselves and poverty in

Table 15.2
Average of Grids of Explanations for Own Low Income
According to Race and Income Source (Welfare or Working)

Category of Informant	Average Value	
	Individual	Social
Black, Welfare	42%	58%
Black, Working	33%	67%
White, Welfare	73%	27%
White, Working	63%	37%
	"We"	"He"	"They"
Black, Welfare	26%	16%	58%
Black, Working	19%	14%	67%
White, Welfare	43%	30%	27%
White, Working	44%	19%	37%
	Thinking	Acting
Black, Welfare	26%	75%
Black, Working	19%	80%
White, Welfare	19%	80%
White, Working	40%	60%

Note: Values may not add up to 100% due to rounding. None can be "generalized" to general public.

general. They seemed to be saying that a good education was not a guarantee of a good income.

Individual / Social

In reference to poverty in general, those on welfare tended to give more weight to the importance of society in causing poverty, while those who worked invested more in individual causes. When it came to their own low income, however, the split was racial. Blacks tended to give more influence to society causing poverty, while whites tended to give more power to the individual.

Racism

Four of the five black informants listed racism as a major cause of poverty in general, but when referring to their own poverty, racism was only listed as a major cause of low income by one informant and by three of the five black informants as a secondary cause.

Divorce

To give a more complete picture of the discussions on poverty presented by the informants, Tables 15.1 and 15.2 also presented a third category, "He," as differentiated from "We" and "They." This category represented the Material Resources argument. The "We" category included the Stress Model, Culture of Poverty and Personal Irresponsibility explanations. The "They" category included the four explanations to the right of the dividing line between individual and social halves of the table. Although the "He" category included several types of causes, often it referred to an individual's activities, but not the poor person, but another person. The most frequent cause of this type was a husband who divorced his wife and left her with no or little income and often in debt. Reference to it was similar in all four categories of informants.

When this third category of causes is factored in, it demonstrated the very low degree to which welfare whites, and to a lesser extent welfare blacks, indicated personal causes for poverty, 17% for whites and 30% for blacks. Once again, the indication of individual causes for poverty for welfare recipients were lower than those whose main income is from work (30% and 17% versus 52% and 39%), and the indication was lowered for whites than for blacks (17% and 39% versus 30% and 52%).

SECTION III
BIBLICAL AND THEOLOGICAL
REFLECTIONS ON POVERTY

This section summarizes Biblical teachings about poverty and the diverse teachings by Christians about poverty. It is presented in four sections: (1) this introduction to the presuppositions and definition of poverty in Chapter 16, (2) Chapter 17 on poverty in the Old Testament, (3) Chapter 18 on what the New Testament says about poverty, and (4) a summary of Christian theology on poverty in Chapter 20.

CHAPTER 16
BIBLICAL DEFINITIONS AND
PRESUPPOSITIONS ABOUT POVERTY

In the Bible, who are the poor, and how is one to act in relation to poverty? After exploring presuppositions, this chapter very briefly outlines common definitions and categorizations of poverty.

Presuppositions about Poverty

It is helpful to consider what presuppositions one may be carrying to this literature. Justo González in the introduction to his presentation of early Christian ideas of money, reviews the Greek, Roman and Hebrew concepts of wealth. As a Christian from North America, the author was surprised by the degree to which his views of wealth seemed to have been more influenced more by Roman concepts than Hebrew or Christian concepts. Especially surprising was the primacy given to the right of private ownership, as someone like Gottfried Dietz and many others would defend today.[1] But Gonzalez explains this is a Roman concept, not Christian.

> The right of an owner, not only to use, but also to abuse or destroy property—with some limitations in the case of slaves—was guaranteed by law and tradition. Indeed, ownership was traditionally defined as the right to use, to enjoy, and to abuse—*jus utendi, jus fruendi, jus abutendi.*[2]

---

[1] Gottfried Dietz, *In Defense of Property* (Baltimore: John Hopkins University Press).

[2] Justo L. Gonzalez, *Faith and Wealth: A History of Early Christian Ideas on the Origin, Significance and Use of Money* (San Francisco: Harper and Row, 1990), 19, emphasis his.

In short, the rights of private property, and the owners' right use it as they saw fit, was the backbone of the Roman legal system. This Roman tradition and jurisprudence, however, did not match the Biblical concepts of private property, nor those among early Christians. The Jews saw the land as the location where their ancestors were buried.

> The land was sacred, not only because it held the sepulchers of the patriarchs of Israel, but also because it was God's land. It had been God's land to give at the time of the conquest, . . . And it remained God's land even while Israel had possession of it.[3]

Care must be taken, therefore, to avoid the unintentional imposition of modern categories and definitions while examining the Biblical text.

Biblical Words and Definition of Poverty

The Lausanne Committee for World Evangelism provided a detailed categorization of the Old Testament concept of poverty through the words used to describe the poor: (1) "the poor as oppressed, downtrodden, humiliated," from the Hebrew verb *'anâ* and adjective *'anî*, (2) "the poor as powerless and diminished," from the verb *dalal*, noun *dal*, and adjective *dallâ*, (3) "the poor as yearning and insistent," from the verb *'abâ*, and the nouns *'abîyônâ* and *'ebyôn*, (4) "the poor as defenseless and open to exploitation," from noun *helekâ*, (5) "poor as needy and in want," from the verb *haser*, and adjectives *haser* and *mahsôr*, (6) "the poor as subject and dependent," from the verb *sakan*, noun *miskenut* and participles *soken* and *misken*, (7) "the poor as diminished and impoverished," from the verb *mûk*, (8) "the poor as destitue and bereft," from the verb *rûsh*, participle *rash* and noun *rêsh*, and (9) "the poor as dispossessed and evicted," from the verb *yarash*.[4]

While this categorization is extensive and valuable, it may portray some bias since the authors seem singularly focused on oppression. Their conclusion clarifies their acceptance of class conflict.

> The poverty of "the wretched of the earth" is clearly shown to be *caused by injustice*. . . .The *economic* poverty they experience is the result of the a prior *social* poverty that is politically structured and

---

[3] Gonzalez, *Faith and Wealth*, 20.

[4]*Thailand Report—Christian Witness to the Urban Poor* (Pattaya, Thailand: Lausanne Committee for World Evangelism, 1980), 22-26.

maintained. Biblically, they are powerless and poor because others are powerful and rich.[5]

The primary New Testament word for poor is *ptochos*, from the verb *ptosso*, meaning to crouch. *Ptochos* meant to be so poor that one was a beggar. Classical Greek also used *penes* or *penichros*, which meant poor as compared to the wealthy—one who had to do manual labor to support one's self. *Penes* was used only once in the New Testament; *ptochos* and its variants were used 38 times.[6]

Stott's categorization of poverty in the Bible is simpler and less strident than the Lausanne Committee's above: (1) "the indigent poor, who are deprived of the basic necessities of life," (2) "the powerless poor, the victims of human oppression," and (3) "the humble poor," who "oppressed by men, they look to God for help, and put their trust in him."[7] These categories almost parallel the senses in which certain Biblical passages concentrate on the subject: the laws of Moses in Leviticus and Deuteronomy which provided basic necessities for all, the humble poor portrayed in the Psalms and the Proverbs and the oppressed poor of the prophets and the Gospels.

Similar discussions of the struggle for food, water and shelter, means of self-support, and feelings of distress, insecurity, shame, and powerlessness are found in secular sources, as well. One of the best is based on World Bank research.[8]

---

[5] Ibid., 27, emphasis theirs.

[6] L. Cohen et al, "Poor," in *New International Dictionary of New Testament Theology*, ed. Colin Brown, 2:820-9 (Grand Rapids, MI: Zondervan, 1976), 821.

[7] John Stott, "Who, then, Are the Poor?" *Christianity Today*, 8 May 1981, 687.

[8] Deepa Narayan, Raj Patel, Kai Schafft, Anne Rademacher and Sarah Koch-Schulte, *Can Anyone Hear Us?* Voices of the Poor Series (New York: Oxford University Press, 2000): 30-65 and Deepa Narayan, Robert Chambers, Meera Kaul Shah, and Patti Petesh, *Crying Out for Change,* Voices of the Poor Series (New York: Oxford University Press, 2000).

CHAPTER 17
OLD TESTAMENT ON POVERTY

Since many texts ascribe wealth as a blessing from God to his favored people, does that mean that poverty is his punishment on evil people? The ability to live in peace, and even be wealthy, appears to be a part of God's promise to Abraham, Isaac, Jacob and his descendents throughout most of the history of the Old Testament and the general "rules of life" contained in the Sapiential literature. But the Old Testament teaching on poverty is much more extensive than this.

Because of this research, certain Biblical texts stand out and need to be incorporated in Christian ministry. These are being presented, not as rules or commandments, but as Biblical examples that show the readers something of God's heart and nature and something of how God wants his people to acts.

The Sabbath
From the end of the very first section of the Bible, the first creation account ending in Genesis 2:2, one sees rest from labor as a part of God's nature. God created a world that "rested" during certain seasons of the year. And He mandated the Sabbath year so that man, beast and land would rest.

Capitalism is caught in a vicious cycle of never ending and ever-increasing work. The continued growth of the economy is dependent on people continuing to buy more products, usually faster than the old ones wear out. In order for the companies to survive, they must continually offer old products at lower prices or new products to encourage consumption. All this puts an increasing pressure on individuals to have more and work more.

It is just this profound difference between the "ruthless efficiencies" many experience at work and the "debilitating inefficiencies of an endlessly expanding welfare state" that led to the "demonization of the poor."[1] Several of the informants interviewed in this research had a different point of view. They pointed out that their economic status was not the most important thing in their life. Several of them, especially single mothers, sacrificed their income in order to nurture their family. Nurturing people was more important to them than producing more and having more.

The author has met numerous men who have confessed that they were very concerned about the amount of time their jobs demanded. They wanted a way out. When it was pointed out that there was, as a last resort, the option to quit, they denied that possibility. It seems that making $60,000 or more per year and working eighty hour weeks was preferable to risking a lower income in order to get fewer hours.

> In the minds of the Old Testament prophets, however, there appears to have been something profoundly destructive and culpable about Israel's tendency toward unrestrained commercial activity. While mankind had been commanded to "work" and to "take care" of the creation (Gen. 2:15), the covenant also required the regular and periodic cessation of this activity in Sabbath observance. Failure to observe the Sabbath, furthermore, seemed inevitably to lead to the oppression of the poor, to the dehumanizing absurdity of idolatry (i.e., the absorption of the worshiper into the object of worship), and to a provocation of the wrath of God against the nation, which ultimately led to judgement.[2]

The choice here is neither workaholism nor welfare, but Godly wisdom and Godly perspective. Noah Snider poses this question: "Is life in a society like Monopoly? Does the game end when one player accumulates all the property titles and wealth? What happens to the rest of us?"[3] James puts commerce in perspective.

---

[1] Craig M. Gay, *With Liberty and Justice for Whom?* (Grand Rapids: Eerdmans, 1991), 239; Ruth Sidel, "The Enemy Within: A Commentary on the Demonization of Difference," *American Journal of Orthopsychiatry* 66, no. 4 (October 1996): 490-95.

[2] Gay, *With Liberty*, 238.

[3] Noah Snider, *When There's No Place Like Home: An Autobiography of the Homeless* (Nashville, TN: Thomas Nelson, 1991), 51.

Now listen you who say, "Today or tomorrow we will go to this or that city, spend a year there, carry on business and make money." Why you do not even know what will happen tomorrow. What is your life? You are a mist that appears for a little while and then vanishes. Instead, you ought to say, "If it is the Lord's will, we will live and do this or that." As it is, you boast and brag. All such boasting is evil. Anyone who knows the good he ought to do and doesn't do it, sins.[4]

The central question is, "Do we trust God enough to defy the ever increasing demands of our economic system to take a break from the consume more / produce more cycle?" The Sabbath is an affront to the ever increasing need to produce more and sell more, and is a glory to God.

Sin

Soon after the introduction of the Sabbath, sin entered the world. Poverty is often related to sin, sometimes in predictable patterns, other times not. Here are some pragmatic conclusions based on experience, interviews and literature review.

1. Many people are poor because they have done stupid and sinful things.

2. Many people are poor because others (parents, husbands, business partners, etc.) have done cruel and sinful things to them.

3. Many people are poor because sinful socio-economic structures have alienated them from the centers of power and resources and given them only enough to make them useful to the power structures.

4. Many middle class and wealthy people are sinners and reprobates, but they inherited wealth or the ability to create wealth anyway.

5. Jesus was a poor man, without sin. While God allowed him to die as a sacrifice for sins, the motive of those who killed him was to stop one whom they perceived to be a threat to their power.

The world is a sinful place, and there is plenty of it to go around for all. The Bible recognizes sin in the poor, especially in the Proverbs.[5] But more common in the Bible is the link between poverty and oppression.

Oppression is viewed as the basic cause of poverty (164 texts). In the case of the other 15 to 20 causes for poverty indicated in the Old

---

[4] James 5:13-17.

[5] Proverbs 6:10, 11:24, 12:11,24, 21:5,17,20, 21:25, 28:19.

Testament, the linquistic link is much less frequent—not more than 20 times.[6]

"Blaming the victim" has been a controversial item for some time and is perhaps the basis of the recent welfare reforms. It may even be true and right, but it has seldom been effective in promoting change in more that one person or family at a time. If blame or sin is going to be the focus of a Christian's ministry with the poor, it should be consistent with God's perspective, which lays the emphasis on the sin of the oppressor.

The Exodus
The Old Testament is dominated by the event of the Exodus, where God had compassion on a suffering people and brought them into a land of freedom and plenty. It dominated the Israelite mind because it is constantly referred back to through out the Old and New Testaments.[7] The Exodus stood as the Israelites' definitive proof that God loved them, for he heard their cries under oppression and freed them! But God's love was not limited to the Israelites. First, as Abraham's descendents, they were to be a conduit of blessing to others.[8] Second, Israel was not the only people he saved from oppression. He had more than one exodus for oppressed people, such as the Ammonites, "descendents of Esau," Caphtorites (Philistines), Arameans and Cushites.[9]

He loved, and loves, all people in need. Once God freed the Israelites from Egyptian slavery, he wanted them to remember what they had suffered and the kind of god he was.

> If a fellow Hebrew, a man or a woman sells himself to you and serves you six years, in the seventh year you must let him go free. . . . Remember that you were slaves in Egypt and the Lord your God redeemed you. That is why I give you this command today.[10]

---

[6] Thomas Hanks, *For God So Loved the Third World* (Maryknoll, NY: Orbis, 1983), quoted in Viv Grigg, *Cry of the Urban Poor* (Monrovia, CA: MARC, 1992), 89.

[7] Ps. 136:10-25; Jer. 2:2-23; Neh. 9:9-12; Acts 7:17-45; Heb. 11:23-31.

[8] Gen. 12:3.

[9] Dt. 2:22-23; Amos 9:7.

[10] Dt. 15:12,15.

It is this identification that God has with the poor that eventually led to Jesus declaring, "I tell you the truth, whatever you did for one of the least of these brothers of mine, you did for me."[11] It also led to God establishing many rules to protect and benefit the poor in their new land, especially the Sabbath Year and the Year of Jubilee as discussed below. Mason categorized these provisions from the Law of Moses.

> 1. A Zero-interest loan will be available, and if the principal has not been repaid by the end of six years the balance will be forgiven (Ex. 22:25; Lev. 25:35-38; Dt. 15:1-11.);
> 2. Israelites committed to slavery for debt-repayment are to be released at the end of six years (assuming the debt has not been fully repaid before then, so that release comes sooner—Lev. 25:47-53)(Ex. 25:21:1-11, Lev. 25:39-43, Dt. 15:12-18);
> 3. An Israelite forced to sell his land for debt-repayment, if the debt has not been repaid by the end of forty-eight years, will have the balance of the debt forgiven and the land returned, to him or his successors (Lev. 25:8-34);
> 4. Each field is to be left fallow every seventh year with the natural growth available for the poor (Ex. 23:10-11; Lev. 25:1-7);
> 5. The gleanings and corners of fields are to be left for the poor, and especially the widows, orphans, and sojourners (Lev. 19:9-10, 23:22; Dt. 24:19-21);
> 6. The third-year tithe will be available for the widows, orphans and sojourners, in addition to the Levites (Dt. 14:28-29, 26:12).[12]

The Years of Sabbath and Jubilee

Exodus 21:2-6 and Leviticus 25 describe a part of God's law for the newly freed Israelites—since God himself owned the land[13] and loaned it freely to the Israelites, they were to regularly share the wealth and the access to wealth! For periods of time varying from seven to forty-nine years, individuals and families had to bear the economic con-sequences of their own actions and those of their ancestors, whether it be for wealth or poverty. But every seven years, all Israelites that had been forced to sell themselves into slavery were released, and every forty-nine years all land was returned to the original owners or his descendants! Thus, the cycle of poverty was broken regularly.

---

[11] Matt. 25:40.

[12] John D. Mason, "Biblical Teaching and Assisting the Poor," in *Best of Theology* vol. 2, ed. J. I. Packer, 295-322 (Carol Streams, IL: Christianity Today, 1987), 300.

[13] Lev. 25:23.

The Jubilee principle of sharing the access to wealth was so important to God and close to his heart that it was part of the reason for Israel's exile.

> You have not obeyed me; you have not proclaimed freedom for your fellow countrymen. So I now proclaim "freedom" for you, declares the LORD—freedom to fall by the sword, plague and famine.[14]

And when Jesus made his inaugural lesson of his ministry in the synagogue in Nazareth, he quoted from Isaiah 61:1, evoking the Jubilee promises.

Three things are important for Christians today. One, sharing the wealth is not solely a communist idea, but God's idea. Communism is one method of sharing the wealth, but certainly not the only one. Two, people need a fresh start every now and then. Three, jobs were a major concern of the informants, but the Jubilee principle emphasizes opportunity and means for self-employment, not jobs. Jobs imply that the capital is already concentrated and the best one can hope for is to sell one's time and energy to a rich person. Jubilee means so much more.

Since the U.S. is not a theocracy, these Sabbath and Jubilee principles are not likely to become law, but less drastic forms of sharing the wealth, fresh starts and self-employment are possible and can be implemented by individual Christians and small groups like churches.

Better than the Tithe

Under the Mosaical law, the tithe went to support the priests and Levites and their work. Beyond the tithe was the responsibility to give help the poor.[15] These were not rules, but showed God's character, which Christians are to imitate. Chewning summarized Biblical teaching by listing five rings of responsibility to help the poor person: (1)

---

[14] Jer. 34:17.

[15] Lev. 25:35-38; Dt. 15:7-11; Prov. 22:9; Matt. 6:19-21, 19:21; John 12:6, 13:29. (For a longer list, see John D. Mason, "Biblical Principles Applied to a Public Welfare Policy," in *Biblical Principles and Public Policy*, ed. Richard C. Chewning, Christians in the Marketplace Series [Colorado Springs: Navpress, 1991], 87.)

the poor person himself, (2) his family, friends and neighbors, (3) the church, (4) businessmen and (5) government.[16]

In the apostolic church, there is no mention of a tithe. There were contributions, and some of the contributions went to support the missionaries,[17] but the emphasis was on giving as a priviledge, not to be limited to prescribed rules, and the distribution of the gifts to the needy.[18]

Trusting God enough to give away our wealth is compounded by the current heavy burden of taxes. A problem for many who want to hand the responsibility of caring for the poor back to the churches and local communities (like in the good old days) is that they do not want to lower federal and state taxes to the levels of that time. These taxes rob local organizations of the funds they had in the good old days.

Ruth's Kinsmen and the Single Mother

In the Bible, there are several types of instructions to God's people on how to provide for women and children. In the Old Testament, it is obvious that marriage was a situation that involved the passing of the wife from her family to that of her husband.[19] If there was a problem and the woman lost her husband's support, she was to be cared for by the family of her husband or return to her home.[20] That does not mean that she simply lived off her husband since that she had numerous responsibilities, such as gleaning and "cottage industries,"[21] but in an agrarian society, survival largely depended on male labor.

The first letter to Timothy had a number of instructions for early Christians. First, a man should work to support his family.[22] Widows were to remarry or be supported by their families.[23] As a last resort, and yet privilege, the church supported widows without family or prospects for a husband so that they may continue their good deeds.[24]

The greatest difficulty is translating principles such as this from a rural, agrarian society to today's industrial or information economy.

---

[16] Richard C. Chewning, ed., *Biblical Principles and Public Policy*, Christians in the Marketplace Series (Colorado Springs: Navpress, 1991), 75-76.

[17] Phil. 4:10-19.

[18] 2 Cor. 8:1-5; Acts 2:44-45, 4:32; Acts 2:45, 4:32-35, 6:1; 2 Cor. 8,9.

[19] Gen. 24:50-51.

[20] Dt. 25:5-9; Ruth 1:8.

[21] Ruth 2:2; Prov. 31:13,16,18-19,24.

[22] 1 Tim. 5:8.

[23] 1 Tim. 5:4,14.

[24] 1 Tim. 5:9-10.

Gleaning was one of the possibilities for the widow in the Old Testament to gain the necessities of life, and it allowed her to work and care for children. Such work is seldom available now, especially for lower paid workers.

Churches need to be consistent. If they teach that a mother's place is in the home, then that applies to the rich, middle class woman, the working poor woman and the welfare poor woman. Churches should not discriminate against welfare mothers who are doing the best they can to raise their children. This means supporting some kind of welfare for single mothers, besides the numerous needs of the working poor treated in other sections.

The Spiritually Needy in the Psalms

Contributing to the third of Stott's list of types of poor people in the Bible, the Psalms are full of references to the poor, but focuses on their only hope, a God who loves them. When King David declares, "For I am poor and needy," the implication is clearly symbolic or spiritual. These passages remind one that in truth everyone is poor before God.

The greatest shortcoming of the conservative church in the North America, however, is to spiritualize every reference to the poor in the Bible and overlook the evil that occurs. All of these references to poverty must be considered in a healthy theology and practice.

Wisdom and Poverty in Proverbs

Since many texts ascribe wealth as a blessing from God to his favored people, does that mean that poverty is his punishment on evil people? The ability to live in peace, and even be wealthy, seem to be a part of the general "rules of life" contained in the Sapiential literature. But, there were many interferences to these general promises and rules such as, the sin of those who stole or acted unjustly (Prov. 13:3; 22:22, 26-27; 28:3), one's own sin which might lead to punishment in order to prompt repentance (Prov. 6:6-11; 13:18; 21:17; 24:30-34; 28:19), the corporate sin of the nation which would lead to punishment in order to prompt national repentance (Prov. 28:28), the decision of God to let Satan tempt one through poverty and oppression (Job 1). Wealth could be blessing from God, as could difficult times.

While many texts, such those below from the prophets, emphasize the oppression that leads to poverty, the Proverbs made it clear that foolishness can also lead to poverty.

God's Prophets in Action

God sent the prophets to indict his people for not following his law and will. While the tendency is to focus on the prophets' preaching against the sin of idolatry, there is considerable, or perhaps even greater, focus on how the Israelites did not follow God's laws to protect the poor.

Just as the ways the prophets denounced this evil were amazingly diverse, so were the ways the poor were mistreated:

(1) The righteous were sold into slavery (Amos 2:6, 8:6; Joel 3:3),

(2) Some of the slaves were submitted to illicit sexual treatment (Amos 2:7,24),

(3) The court and justice system were perverted against the poor (Amos 2:7, 5:7,10,12; Micah 3:1,9,11, 7:3; Zech. 5:3-4, 7:8, 8:4, 8:16; Hab. 2:6-8; Hosea 10:3-4),

(4) Property of the poor was confiscated illegally (Amos 5:11; Hab. 2:6-8),

(5) The poverty of the poor was used to provide luxury for the rich (Amos 2:7, 6:1-7, 8:4),

(6) The commercial powers cheated and took advantage of the poor (Amos 8:5; Micah 6:10,11; Hab. 2:9-11; Hosea 12:7),

(7) The stranger, widow and orphan were abused (Micah 2:8,9; Mal. 3:5; Zech. 7:10),

(8) Laborers were defrauded of their wages (Mal. 3:5),

(9) Common laws of humanity were disregarded (Amos 1:6,9,11; Obad. 10-14; Zeph. 2:8-11),

(10) The flesh of the poor was torn and blood shed to acheive this (Micah 3:2,3; Hab. 2:12-14).

Because of the lack of repentance for this evil, Jeremiah announced Israel's coming punishment,

> You have not obeyed me; you have not proclaimed freedom for your fellow countrymen. So I now proclaim "freedom" for you, declares the LORD—freedom to fall by the sword, plague and famine.[25]

Because the people did not free the oppressed, they themselves were to become the oppressed.

The response of the Israelites was to mistreat and kill their prophets.[26] Yet, God held the prophets responsible to continue to warn the people of the consequences of their evil actions.

---

[25] Jer. 34:17.

When I say to a wicked man, "You will surely die," and you do not warn him or speak out to dissuade him from his evil ways to save his life, that wicked man will die for his sin, and I will hold you accountable for his blood.[27]

While the miraculous ability to foresee the future may have discontinued with the completion of the scriptures, the prophetic function of recognizing sin and trying to persuade people to repent has not changed. The church needs to listen and respond responsibly to her prophets rather than persecute and alienate them. This is for the good of the church, the prophet and the poor.

Community Service According to Nehemiah

Nehemiah, that little known builder near the end of the Old Testament period, is a good example of godly community development that could be followed today. Many have extolled Nehemiah's excellent example of leadership, but his story is also an example of the mind games that the Devil tries to play in godly people's minds when they try to help people in distress. It is barriers such as a warped vision of reality, fear, greed, ego-centrism, compartmentalized religion and short term committment that seem to hinder so many Christians in their outreach to the needy, and it is in these areas that Nehemiah is such a good example.[28]

Conclusion

The Old Testament offers a rich source of information on poverty. It is not simplistic, but defends the idea that poverty can result from a multitude of causes and sources. Sometimes the poor person is the cause; often it is the unjust. While the tendency is to treat poverty in individualistic terms, the laws of Moses clarify that often poverty is caused by structural injustice. These laws structure society to avoid injustice and hold the unjust one accountable.

---

[26] Heb. 11:35-38.

[27] Ezek. 3:18.

[28] Michael L. Landon, "Community Development According to Nehemiah," *Restoration Quarterly* 42 #1 (Spring 2000): 47-51.

CHAPTER 18
THE NEW TESTAMENT ON POVERTY

The New Testament is rich with references to wealth and poverty. A few of the most important points for this study include Jesus' life and that of the early church and the connection between salvation by grace and poverty.

Jesus' Life

Jesus was born into a poor family, grew to be a poor man and spent most of his ministry with the common person. To announce the beginning of his ministry, he referred to the Year of Jubilee by quoting from Isaiah 61:1.

> The Spirit of the Lord is on me,
>> because he has anointed me
>> to preach good news to the poor.
> He has sent me to proclaim freedom for the prisoners
>> and recovery of sight for the blind,
>> to release the oppressed,
>> to proclaim the year of the Lord's favor.[1]

While it is true that Jesus did not come to begin a new political reign, but to "seek and save the lost," he messed with the socio-economic system! He started an economic revolution through the *koinania* of the early church. He threatened the powerful through such parables as the good Samaritan[2] and the shrewd manager.[3] "The Pharisees, who

---

[1] Luke 4:18-19.
[2] Luke 10.
[3] Luke 16:1-13.

loved money, heard all this and were sneering at Jesus."[4] God allowed Jesus to be killed in order to pay for man's sins, but the motive of those who killed him was to protect their power.

The mainstream evangelical church has hidden behind the spiritualization of Jesus for far too long. It takes passages such as "Blessed are you who are poor"[5] and spiritualizes it to mean the same thing as "Blessed are the poor in spirit,"[6] a much more comfortable lesson for middle class believers. It ignores lessons such as Luke 6:24-26, "But woe to you who are rich, . . ."

Brown suggests that to truly take the Bible seriously, "we must be in dialogue not only with the Bible, but also with Christians in other part of the world who read the Bible in a very different way."[7] Sometimes third world Christians think that people like us read the Bible from the vantage point of our privilege and comfort and screen out those parts that threaten us. They point out that the basic viewpoint of the biblical writers is that of victims, those who have been cruelly used by society, the poor and oppressed. Is that what the Bible is really all about? Enough third world Christians are saying so, and are living changed lives as a result, to impel us to explore the matter and see whether there might be a new word for us as well.[8]

Miguez-Bonino clarifies that this is not a "theology of poverty," but "a theology which 'thinks' the Gospel from within a conscious and lucid option for the poor." It includes the perspective, priorities and "goal and purpose" of the poor.[9]

The Early Church and the Poor

The early church obviously included a great many needy people and served needy people. The Jerusalem church had so many poor people that sharing the wealth,[10] especially feeding the needy widows,[11] was a necessary action for survival. Later on, Paul gave instructions for the care for needy widows, either through their families or the

---

[4] Luke 16:14.

[5] Luke 6:20.

[6] Matthew 5:3.

[7] Robert M. Brown, *Unexpected News: Reading the Bible with Third World Eyes* (Philadelphia: Westminster Press, 1984), 13.

[8] Ibid., 14.

[9] Jose Miguez-Bonino, "Doing Theology in the Context of the Struggles of the Poor." *Mid-Stream* 20 (1981): 370-1.

[10] Acts 2:42-47; 4:32-37.

[11] Acts 6.

church.[12] And James demanded dignity and service to the poor,[13] which may have been in danger as the church began to spread into the greater Greco-Roman world.[14] This kind of regard for the poor was a social and economic revolution.

As Jesus had demanded earlier, the apostles didn't depend on purses, but on the Lord.[15] They were poor by choice, in order to better serve.[16]

Salvation by Grace

The theological implications of how the "unworthy" are treated in many conservative churches is scary. It is rather astonishing that a people who so strongly contest for "salvation by grace" can be so strongly "respected by works." Many presume that they got where they are because of their good character, while the poor got where they are because of their faulty character. One informant reported that Christian organizations didn't know what to do with an intelligent poor person who won't conform to their patronizing and belittling attitude.

The church often acts like the Israelites who so prized what God did for them in the Exodus and their status as God's people, yet they refused to liberate others in need.

> You have not obeyed me; you have not proclaimed freedom for your fellow countrymen. So I now proclaim "freedom" for you, declares the LORD—freedom to fall by the sword, plague and famine.[17]

The Christian today who is a sinner, yet saved by God's grace, but refuses to be gracious with other unworthy sinners may be risking the same result as the Israelites, freed from slavery in Egypt, but now slave holders.

Don't be afraid to "re-evangelize the church."[18] Churches that are more ontological than practical, disconnected from their community, who treat other people as categories rather than individuals created by

---

[12] 1 Timothy 5:3-16.

[13] James 1:27; 2:1-12.

[14] I Corinthians 6:1; 8:4 and11:21 seem to refer to the wealthy church members disregarding the good of their poorer brothers.

[15] Acts 3:6.

[16] Philippians 4:12; II Corinthians 11:7.

[17] Jeremiah 34:17.

[18] J. N. J. Kritzinger, "Liberating Mission in South Africa" *Missionalia* 18 #1 (1990): 45.

God and at the same reject community in favor of extreme individualism for themselves, need to be re-acquainted with the good news of
the Kingdom of God.[19] Churches' "common inventory of besetting
sins" must change.[20] Exploitation, greed, and violence are just as evil as
the individualistic list of things like, stealing, gambling, drunkenness,
profanity, murder and adultery.

Dawson's "Instructions to a Demon" describes all too well how
the church has fought itself into uselessness over nuances of truth
while the devil strengthened strongholds in our nation.[21] Müntzer
asserted, "The defeat of the 'world' within means at the same time and
in the same process the defeat of the world without."[22] Churches must
arm itself with truth, righteousness, peace, faith, salvation and the spirit
to fight against the "rulers, authorities and powers of this dark world,
and against the spiritual forces of evil in heavenly places."[23]

---

[19] Mark 1:14-15.

[20] Stephen C. Mott, *Biblical Ethics and Social Change* (New York: Oxford
University Press, 1982), 17.

[21] John Dawson, *Healing America's Wounds* (Ventura, CA: Regal Books,
1994), 106-7.

[22] Hans-Jurgen Goertz, "The Mystic with the Hammer, Thomas Muntzer's
Theological Basis for Revolution" in *Mennonite Quarterly Review* L (1976):
101.

[23] Ephesians 6:12-17.

CHAPTER 19
CHRISTIAN REFLECTIONS ON POVERTY

This chapter quickly reviews some early and medieval writings on wealth and poverty and then concentrates on modern teachings on poverty by Christians.

Early Church Fathers on Wealth

Uhlhorn summarized the early church's relationship with the poor:

> It was when misery became greater and greater in the perishing world, when the arm of the state was more and more paralyzed, when the authorities no longer offered assistance to the poor and the oppressed, ney, themselves took a part in oppressing and exhausting them, that the church became on a grand scale the refuge of all the oppressed and suffering.[1]

The church from its beginnings in Jerusalem helped the poor through the love feasts, official status of widows, assistance in finding jobs and regular collection for the poor, which were often stored at the bishop's house for distribution.[2]

González summarizes a number of themes about poverty that appeared in the writings of the church fathers.

---

[1] Gerhad Uhlhorn, *Christian Charity in the Ancient Church* (New York: Scribner's, 1883), 362 quoted in Hans Schwartz, "God's Cause for the Poor in Light of the Christian Tradition" in *God and Global Justice*, 169-84, ed. Frederick Ferré and Rita H. Mataragon (New York: Paragon House, 1985), 179.

[2] Hans Schwarz, "God's Cause for the Poor in Light of the Christian Tradition," in *God and Global Justice*, 169-84, ed. Frederick Ferré and Rita H. Mataragon (New York: Paragon House, 1985), 179-80.

1. All the writers, from New Testament texts through Augustine, assumed that faith influenced wealth.

2. All condemned usury.

3. A theme borrowed from pagan text was that the "rich are in truth poor in virtue and poor in joy."

4. When one gives to the poor, one is lending to God.

5. The rich are at a disadvantage when entering the kingdom of God.

6. One who can help another and doesn't do so, becomes guilty of the fate of the injured.

7. All things, including wealth, are seen as good.

8. Yet, the accumulation of wealth is evil. Not necessarily because things are evil, but the love of things is.

9. The holding of private property was unanimously assumed, but understood differently than the Roman concept. All property ultimately belonged to God, and private stewardship of it was limited by its proper use.

10. The sharing exemplified in the Jerusalem church continued well into the second century and in some forms into the third. What did change was a transfer from the early forms of *koinonia* to almsgiving, although almsgiving was understood to be the giving away of all extra wealth, not just loose change to beggars.[3]

Medieval and Reformation Views of Wealth

The medieval church seemed to have a split personality over money. On one hand it seemed to have been influenced by ascetic movements and began to view money as unspiritual. Commercial activity was particularly viewed with suspicion. But at the same, the church began to institutionalize almsgivings in order to help the poor.[4]

The reformers rebelled against this "glorification of poverty." Money became, not a part of the Fall, but a part of creation and a tool for the creation of wealth. Even the prohibition of usuary was questioned by Calvin. According to Muether, Wesley urged, "Make as much as you can, save as much as you can, and give as much as you

---

[3] Justo L. González, *Faith and Wealth: A History of Early Christian Ideas on the Origin, Significance and Use of Money* (San Francisco: Harper and Row, 1990), 225-28.

[4] John R. Muether, "Money and the Bible," *Christian History* 6, no. 2 (1987): 7.

can."[5] This view was brought to the American colonies by the Puritans and became known as the Protestant Work Ethic. It also led to Weber's famous thesis linking Calvinism and capitalism.[6]

This hardy embracing of wealth, commerce and interest was not without dissent. The Anabaptists argued for a further reformation that included the *koinonia* sharing of the early church. Themselves embracing work and virtue like the other Protestants, the Anabaptist also insisted on simple living, lack of pretentiousness and compassion for the poor. Most allowed private property, but a few groups insisted on communal ownership.[7]

Current Theological Debates on Poverty

Petersen, in a recent article entitled "Modern Voices: The Christian and Money," presented the contemporary views of money as they are being presented to North American church members. His categories included: (1) the simple living movement, (2) the missions movement (summarized by "give till it hurts"), (3) Liberation theology, (4) theonomy (only Christians know how to use money correctly, so they should get as much as possible), (5) the health and wealth gospel (God blesses good people with good things), (6) neo-conservatives (anti-socialists), (7) the U.S. Catholic bishops' directions to rethink the moral implications of money and (8) Ellul's systemic view of money and concern with idolatry.[8] From these categories, three deserve fuller discussion because they have been major participants in the discussion on causes of poverty: the simple living movement, neo-conservatives and Liberation Theology.

The Simple Living Movement

According to Petersen, Ronald Sider has always been the major spokesperson for the simple living movement.[9] The movement has always had two prongs—personal and social applications. The Anabaptist tradition and Richard Foster have provided the personal application, while Ron Sider and magazines such as *The Other Side* and

---

[5] Ibid., 7-8.

[6] Ibid., 8.

[7] Ibid.

[8] Randy Petersen, "Modern Voices: The Christian and Money," *Christian History* 6, no. 2 (1987): 28-33.

[9] Ibid., 28.

Sojourners led the social application.[10] And Anabaptists are increasing speaking out on the social applications as well. The first part of this section outlines Sider's arguments for simple living. The second part discusses the social philosophy that supports this movement.

Sider definitely speaks from a North American point of view. To him, the primary problem for a North American Christian is, "How can this be? How can so many be in such desperate poverty while I and so many other Christians live lives of luxury?"[11]

Sider's most prominent book, *Rich Christians in an Age of Hunger*, has three parts: a brief introduction to the "widening chasm" between the rich and the poor, a Bible study on the poor and possessions and suggestions for implementing change. The Bible study section deals with: (1) God's relationship with the poor, (2) economic principles of the Bible, such as the Jubilee, Sabbath Year, tithing and gleaning, Jerusalem koinania, (3) Biblical perspectives on private property and (4) structural evil.[12] Much of the details of Sider's presentation is similar to the Bible study above.

Sider's Bible study on structural evil makes clear a link with other theologians who are studying the "powers," references in Pauline literature normally taken to be about Satan and demons. These writings, though they do not discuss poverty, demonstrate the social philosophy of the simple living movement. Berkhof prompted this discussion through his *Christ and the Powers*.[13] Since then the principal arguments have been written by Yoder, Mouw and Mott.

Yoder uses Colossians 1:15-17 to transfer the concept of thrones, powers, rulers and authorities from the demonic to the structural. According to Yoder, since the word "subsist" has the same root as systematize, this could mean that everything that Christ maintains united is the world powers. It is the reign of order among creatures, order that in its original intentions is a divine gift.[14] This order, of course, fell. Thus, Yoder depersonalizes (demythologizes) the powers and authorities from the older concept of demons to simply world social structures, and it is these world structures that perpetuate earthly evil.

---

[10] Ibid., 28-29.

[11] Ibid., 29.

[12] Ron Sider, *Rich Christians in an Age of Hunger,* revised and expanded ed. (Downers Grove, IL: InterVarsity 1984), 53-160.

[13] Hendrik Berkof, *Christ and the Powers* (Scottdale: Herald 1962).

[14] John H. Yoder, *The Politics of Jesus* (Grand Rapids: Eerdmans, 1972), 143.

Mouw seems to maintain some concept of personal powers, but also demythologizes the powers and emphasizes this element to the degree that they are relegated to little more than earthly social systems. His emphasis on human evil, however, includes both the individual and systemic causes. The real cause of earthly evil is not the powers, but the human tendency for idolatry, whether individual or systemic.

> We might think of the Powers, then as having to do with various forces, spheres, and patterns of our lives which present themselves to us as possible objects of idolatry. A nation or race can become an object of ultimate loyalty, as can sexual enjoyment, humanitarians pursuits or even an religious commitment. . . . Thus, we are dealing with the domains of the Powers when we are taking an inventory of various possible objects of human idolatry.[15]

The personal choice for idolatry caused an incorporation of idolatry into the social fabric.

> The two are related in that the Bible pictures all injustice and oppression as stemming from a posture of personal rebellion against the Creator. Corporate injustice and the neurotic patterns that characterize collective interaction are results of the institutionalization of this personal rebellion. . . . But these institutionalizations of the personal sinful project can come to have a life of their own. . . . If the manipulative patterns which are built into the very structures of social relationships are not changed, all of the effects of sin have of been challenged—and it may be that as a result many "hearts" will not be capable of adequate "change".[16]

Thus, while Mouw focuses on the structural form of human evil and its ongoing nature, he sees the root of human evil to be an individual problem, idolatry. Mouw seems to be addressing his book to the individual with the purpose of encouraging him to engage his community in reflection and action about the problems of society and possible structural solutions.

Although Mott also discusses the powers and the *stoicheia* (elements which had been personalized by New Testament times), he does not try "to settle the cosmological question of whether angels and demons should be demythologized but rather to come to terms with the

---

[15] Richard J. Mouw, *Politics and the Biblical Drama* (Grand Rapids: Baker, 1976), 89.
[16] Ibid., 49-50.

social material to which their biblical existence points."[17] The key
Biblical term about social evil is *cosmos*.

> A basic way of describing evil in the New Testament uses the term
> cosmos, "the world." This word refers to the order of society and
> indicates that evil has a social and political character beyond the
> isolated actions of individuals. . . . The cosmos, a more pervasive
> theme in the New Testament than the powers, represents the social
> structuring of evil without necessitating recourse to the symbolism of
> supernatural personages.[18]

In sum, the evangelicals differentiate between the source and
motor of social evil. For Yoder, the source of social evil is the powers;
Mouw, humans; and Mott, the cosmos. The motor, however, is
structural for all—Yoder, structural powers; Mouw, structural idolatry;
and Mott, the structured cosmos. O'Brien is an important critic who
accuses these three and other of "demythologizing" or depersonalizing
the powers.[19]

Because of this emphasis on social evil and perhaps in reaction to
the extreme individualism of the evangelical church, the simple living
movement has tended to emphasize the structural causes of poverty.

Neo-Conservatives

Prominent literature in this category includes David Chilton,
Rousas J. Rushdoony, Greg Bahnsen, Gary North and Michael
Novak.[20] Gary North serves as a good example of this group since, as
Petersen puts it, "the theonomists encamp at Mt. Sinai (Exodus 20)."[21]

The neo-conservatives are the religious version of the Ethos expla-
nation for poverty discussed later. The Ethos arguments tends to defend
North American Protestant Capitalism against the attacks by Liberation
Theology, but North returns to an even older way of organizing life
than the United States of 1950's—the Ten Commandments. When
North advocates an ethical basis for wealth and poverty, at first reading

---

[17] Stephen C. Mott, *Biblical Ethics and Social Change* (New York: Oxford
University Press, 1982), 10.

[18] Ibid., 4,10.

[19] P. T. O'Brien, "Principalities and Powers" in *Biblical Interpretation,* ed. D.
A. Carson (New York: Nelson, 1985), 110-50.

[20] Petersen, "Modern Voices," 29.

[21] Ibid., 31.

he seems to be advocating personal / familial responsibilities to create wealth and therefore avoid poverty.

> Murray's conclusion is eloquent, and it gets right to the point: the presence of long-term poverty is not primarily a function of family income. It is a function of morality, time, perspective, and faith regarding economic causes and effects.[22]

> There is a predictable, lawful relationship between personal industriousness and wealth, between laziness and poverty.[23]

In order to preserve family capital over time, godly parents must train their children to follow the ethical standards of the Bible. The biblical basis for long-term expansion of family capital is ethical: character and competence.[24]

While his emphasis on ethics is obvious, one must remember that his perspective is social rather than personal. One of North's bestsellers, *The Sinai Strategy*, is not a personal strategy for wellbeing, but a call to return to the ethical / political strategy originally produced for the nation of Israel, and now advocated as a means to renew North American society. "At the very least, we should find in the ten commandments laws that apply to civil government and economics."[25]

> What the ten commandments set forth is a strategy. This strategy is a strategy for dominion. . . . But the Decalogue itself is the master plan, the blueprint for biblical social order.[26]

Since both the neo-conservatives and the simple living movement point to the Law of Moses as a socio-economic model for today, what is the difference then between them? (1) The simple living movement tends to be very much a counter-cultural movement within the American experience, very suspicious of social structures in general and somewhat critical of capitalism. The neo-conservatives tend to talk about returning to the good old days of Christian America. They tend to be very affirming of social structures and capitalism, at least the

---

[22] Gary North, *The Sinai Strategy* (Tyler, TX: Institute for Christian Economics, 1986), 132.

[23] Ibid., 141.

[24] Ibid., 98.

[25] Ibid., 4.

[26] Ibid., 7.

North American experience of them. (2) The neo-conservatives would be accused by the simple living movement of reading North American capitalism into the Biblical text. The simple living movement does not see much capitalism in the Bible, nor private property, but instead private stewardship.

Liberation Theology

Liberation theologians go beyond criticism of capitalism to being full-blown socialists. They link poverty with system and sin, but one must be careful to clarify that the sin is not of the poor, but of the society—"[p]overty is a social sin that God does not will, . . ."[27] System is linked with poverty because, according to them, poverty is caused by unjust social systems, of which the primary is the economic system. Liberation Theology is dependent on Marxist social presuppositions that require that the mode of production be responsible for the structuring of the rest of society. This is further discussed later under Dependency Theory.

Prominent liberation theologians are passionate in their repeated linking poverty with injustice, oppression, idolatry and even death.

> The poor is the sub-product of the system in which we live and for which we are responsible. He is the marginalized from our social and cultural world. Even more, the poor is the oppressed, the exploited, the proletariat, the one deprived of the fruit of his work, the one plundered of his humanness.[28]

> The poor are poor because they are exploited or rejected by a perverse economic organization, as in our capitalism. This is the exploitative and exclusive system. For this very reason, the poor is oppressed and suffers. He is maintained under the system or out of it. Such is the true explanation of the poverty of the poor.[29]

> It deals first of all with an alternative in which in the name of some divinities, explicit religiously or in secularized visions such as

---

[27] Leonardo Boff, *Jesus Christ Libertador*, tran. Patrick Hughes (Maryknoll, NY: Orbis, 1978), 270.

[28] Gustavo Gutierrez, *Teologia da Libertação*, 6th ed., trans. by Jorge Soares (Petrópolis, Brazil: Vozes, 1986), 256. Note: this and other quotes from works in Portuguese are translated by Michael Landon.

[29] Jorge Pixley and Clodovis Boff, *Opção Pelos Pobres* (Petrópolis, Brazil: Vozes, 1986), 21.

"democracy," "private property" and national security," death is given to men, dehumanizing them and impoverishing them.[30]

The current ruling structures, dependent capitalism and national security, . . . act as true gods and as their own worship. . . . And they have their own worship because they demand daily sacrifices of the majorities and the violent sacrifice of those who fight against them. This deity has the necessity of victims to subsist and produces them by necessity.[31]

Liberation theologians produce this interpretation of reality, and call it sin—sin of the social structures. Clodovis Boff defines social or structural sin as "a human evil which acquires an existence exterior to the individual and which imposes itself on the consciousness of the individual."[32] The unjust structures of the society are to the society what lust is to the individual. Moser explains that structural sin is perpetuated in the society through "means, models, ideas, values, the collective mentality."[33]

Structural sin is not the same as collective sin (which is the collective consequences of the sin of the individual) nor original sin, although the latter serves as stepping off spot.[34] An example of collective sin is Korah's rebellion against Moses and God in Numbers 16. Korah, Dathin and Abiram sinned, but their entire families and households suffered the consequences. Structural sin, however, involves sin which penetrates the social structure so that groups of people and institutions routinely carry out sinful activities. Some examples may be: (1) expected perrogatives of a king (I Sam. 8), (2) the expected methods and results of war such as slavery, killing kinsmen and killing pregnant women (Amos 1:9-13), (3) the alliance between the military,

---

[30] Jon Sobrino, *Ressurreição da Verdadeira Igreja*, trans. by Luiz Joao Gaio (São Paulo, Brazil: Edições Loyola, 1982), 155.

[31] Ibid., 173.

[32] Clodovis Boff, "O Pecado Social," *Revista Ecclesiastica Brasileira* 37 (1977): 693; similar definition in Arthur Rich, "Imperativos Objetivos de la Economia y Pecado Estrutural," trans. and condensed by Carlos Gonzalez, *Selecciones de Teologia* 24 (January-March 1985): 37.

[33] Antonio Moser, "Pecado e Condicionamentos Humanos" in *Grande Sinal 1975*, 339-50 (Petropolis, Brazil: Vozes), 346. Normally this would be percieved as ethos, but Marx insists that mode of production forms the ethos.

[34] Antonio Moser, "Mais Desafios para a Teologia do Pecado," *Revista Eclesiástica Brasileira* 40 (December 1980): 687.

commercial and religious establishments in Israel,[35] (4) the money changers and merchants in the Temple during the time of Jesus (Mark 11), (5) the alliance between the Roman governors and the Sanhedren "to maintain peace" in Judea (Luke 20; Mark 12:13-17; Matt. 27:62-22) and (6) the religious establishment which turned the Sabbath into a burden instead of a joy (Matt. 11:25-12:14).

Moser clarifies that "situation of sin," "social sin" and "structural sin" all refer to the same basic concept.[36] He further clarifies that communitarian sin refers to the primary social relationships (personal relationships in the family and community), while social or structural sin refer to the secondary social relationships (economy, political organization, etc.).[37] Moser affirms that reality is not a matter of either personal sin or structural sin, but a dialectical continuum of personal and structural sin.[38]

The roots for this structural sin have various explanations. Boff begins by defining sin as "unlove," a "negative relationship with God," but does little to relate it to social sin.[39] Moser defines sin as "negation of the Kingdom."[40] It seems, therefore, that denying God takes a back seat to denying the Kingdom since "sin to Jesus is not put primarily as negation of God, but as formal negation of the Kingdom of God."[41] Rich has yet another way to define sin and social sin. Love is defined as "living in dialogue" with God and men, meaning that one lives considerately. A monologue is evil, and sin is defined as living in monologue.

> Since loving means not living for yourself, but primarily with and for the other. The other which is God and the other which is man. And all this means that the essence of love is a dialoguing existence, a life in dialogue with God and with God and with all those whom we meet.[42]

---

[35] Michael L. Landon, "A Missiological Interpretation of Amos 2:6-16: An Example of Theology on Edge," paper read at the Christian Scholars Conference, Nashville, TN, July 1996 (available from Lipscomb University).

[36] Moser, "Mais Desafios," 689.

[37] Ibid., 684.

[38] Ibid., 690.

[39] Boff, "O Pecado Social," 676, 678.

[40] Moser, "Mais Desafios," 682.

[41] Ibid., 686.

[42] Rich, "Imperativos Objetivos," 34.

But one doesn't live in isolation. The Biblical story of original sin makes it clear that to Rich that sin is more than just personal sin, and today, humans experience both personal and structural sin.[43] In fact, it's inescapable.[44]

Reflections on the Theologies of Poverty

Below are some reactions to, reflections on and conclusions from this Biblical and theological literature. They may seem simplistic, but they represent some profound changes compared to how the author viewed poverty.

Interpretation and Experience

The author was raised with a belief in the ability of humans to read the Bible for details on church life and replicate those patterns today, "standing," as it were, "outside history as a self-made" church.[45] Recent works have shown that there are all sorts of presuppositions embedded in such a belief.[46] This "illusion of innocence" was typical of most theology based on Positivism. The more useful model of Biblical interpretation now is the "hermeneutical circle" which recognizes the importance of the interpreter's context in the process of doing theology.[47]

The author's own theories of poverty and understanding of the Bible and God changed dramatically as he experienced working class life in the United States, a middle class education and salary, personal relationships with poor families in Brazil, studies with Liberation theologians and activists, the financial strain of being a returned missionary and doctoral student and then again on a middle class salary.

---

[43] Ibid., 35.

[44] Ibid., 43.

[45] Walter Brueggemann, *The Prophetic Imagination* 2nd ed (Minneapolis, MN: Fortress, 2001), 37.

[46] Richard T. Hughes and C. Leonard Allen, *Discovering Our Roots: The Ancestry of Churches of Christ* (Abilene, TX: ACU Press, 1988); Richard T. Hughes and C. Leonard Allen, *Illusions of Innocence: Protestant Primitivism in America, 1630-1875* (Chicago: University of Chicago Press, 1988); C. Leonard Allen, Randy T. Hughes, and Michael R. Weed, *The Worldly Church* (Abilene, TX: ACU Press, 1988).

[47] Anthony Thiselton, *Two Horizons* (Grand Rapids: Eerdmans, 1980), 103; John Stott, *Between Two Worlds* (Grand Rapids: Eerdmans, 1982), 106, 137-144; Boff, *Jesus Cristo Libertador*, 228.

It seems clear that the neo-conservatives and liberation theologians are each interpreting poverty, capitalism and the Bible from their own very different contexts, and so their results are different. They seem to be talking right past each other with little real communication, as would be expected from paradigm theory.[48] What is more important is that since their theology is experienced-based and their experience is limited, their theology is partial. But they often assume that their theology is universal.

Two things could help this conflict. One, experience in more than one culture is a valuable asset when studying people and the Bible. If only these two groups could exchange contexts and ministries for a few years! Two, some humility could go a long ways, humility enough to use a "meta-theology," a procedure for evaluating theology, such as the one suggested by Hiebert.[49]

God and the Poor

The true, living God is a god who has a special affection for the poor and afflicted. That was demonstrated time and again in the Bible, but primarily through the incarnation. Out of all the options, Jesus chose to come as a poor man "to preach good news to the poor."[50] If Christians are to be true disciples of Christ, then they must "be transformed into his likeness."[51]

Biblical Understanding of Poverty

North American Christians tend to categorize poor people into the "deserving poor" and the "undeserving poor." Even then, the point of reference is the middle-class Christian thinking about helping a poor person, not the poor person. Stott's categories of Biblical references to the poor seem to be a much overall description. His categorization includes: (a) "the indigent poor, who are deprived of the basic necessities of life," (b) "the powerless poor, the victims of human oppression," and (c) "the humble poor," who "oppressed by men, they look to God for help, and put their trust in him."[52]

---

[48] Thomas S. Kuhn, *The Structure of Scientific Revolutions*, 2nd ed. (Chicago: University of Chicago Press, 1970), 147-48.

[49] Paul G. Hiebert, *Anthropological Reflections on Missiological Issues* (Grand Rapids: Baker Book House, 1994), 100.

[50] Luke 4:18.

[51] 2 Co. 3:18.

[52] John Stott, "Who, then, are the Poor?" *Christianity Today*, 8 May 1981, 687.

What Stott leaves unspoken is that a poor person may fit one of these categories, but more likely, all three at the same time. Thus, there aren't necessarily three types of poor people in the Bible, but three ways of looking at the same poverty: in relation to need or the material world, in relation to other humans and in relation to God. The focus has changed from the potential and timid charity giver to the poor person, and it has changed from that one way relationship to a more complex set of relationships.

As long as the poor person is the "other," the church will never be effective in ministry with the poor, and even more importantly, never be transformed into Jesus' image, for He chose to incarnate as a poor person.

SECTION IV
IMPLICATIONS AND
SUGGESTIONS FOR ACTION

This section summarizes the implications of this study for Christian involvement in poor people's lives and makes suggestions on how to work with poor people for mutual benefit.

CHAPTER 20
IMPLICATIONS FOR CHRISTIANS

According to Yin, the strength of the case studies, such as Section II, is the implications for theory and organizational policies.[1] The first section will introduce the chapter by presenting four issues from the findings that seem to be most important to the church. This will be followed by some theological implications and suggestions for what churches can do with and for lower income people. The suggestions are discussed separately from the issues because poverty can be a holistic condition, and any one of the issues discussed below may require a variety of types of suggestions (economic planning, political influence, building understanding through relationships). Thus, there is no one solution for each of the issues below, only multiple suggestions that may or may not apply to each issue.

Issues for the Church

A part of what scares the church away from more ministry with the poor is the enormity and complexity of the problem. From this research, however, four issues have arisen that seem to be the most important to church and also the most likely ways to improve the life of those with low income. Perhaps by concentrating on these four opportunities, the church can begin to learn how to deal with other facets of poverty.

First, the majority of the informants who were on welfare displayed a strong anger towards churches. As long as this continues, it will block growth and service to the poor. Second, a high percentage of

---

[1] Robert K. Yin, *Case Study Research* (Newbury Park, CA: SAGE Publications, 1989), 38-40.

the poor are single mothers, caused mainly by divorce and sex outside of marriage. The church isn't sure what to do since it doesn't condone much of what is causing this single motherhood, neither illegitimate sex nor many of the divorces, but ignoring the problem and hoping it will go away has only caused it to grow. Third, in our society, jobs and benefits are the primary ways of creating wealth and are the key to the financial growth of poor families. Fourth, several of the informants admitted to being moderately to severely depressed.

Those on Welfare Are Angry with Churches

As is almost expected in the southern U.S., all of the informants had or had had relationships with churches. Three of the eight families indicated that they were satisfied with their churches and saw them as a place for help or at least comfort in times of need. These three were all working poor. The majority of the poor, however, and all of the welfare poor, were angry with churches. One was unsatisfied because of the scandals associated with ministers, but the other four were unhappy with the way churches treated them and poor people in general.

Many of the poor read their Bibles and recognized selective Bible reading when they saw it. The Bible is full of injunctions to help the poor,[2] but American churches tend to just help the poor who are far away.

> I mean like, like if, I think that my church can send thousands of dollars to Mexico every month, or two thousand dollars here, two thousand dollars over there, why can't we spend a couple of those thousand, and take care of our people in our own church?

Demonization of the Welfare Poor

Sidel and Withorn discuss the demonization of welfare recipients. "Virtually all of the ills afflicting American society are being attributed to single-mother families."[3]

> Poor women are characterized by their "dependence," an absolute negative, a polar opposite from that valued American characteristic, "independence." This label presumes that *they* are "dependent," that *they* passively rely on the government for their day-to-day needs *we,*

---

[2] James 1:27.

[3] Ruth Sidel, "The Enemy Within: A Commentary on the Demonization of Difference," *American Journal of Orthopsychiatry* 66, no. 4 (October 1996): 490-495.

the rest of us, are "independent," "pull ourselves up by our own boot-straps," are out there "on our own."[4]

How do churches demonize the poor, especially those on welfare? They trivialize their problems by arrogantly instructing them on how to live on $400 a month. They ignore them or push them away by leaving signs on our doors saying to go to the cooperative food bank or traveler's aid, or by the grimace on one's face when a poor person asks for help. Church representatives grill them to weed out the "deserving from the undeserving," assuming they're guilty until proven innocent. Church members talk freely and angrily about "those people," while never realizing how close all are to their position. The church patronizes them, as when the author heard one minister declare

> There's little difference between us. My wife has to work to supplement my [$60,000 a year] salary, so a poor wife must work to supplement her husband's $12,000 salary. She must work, like my wife does, instead of receiving welfare.

Are both wives really under the same pressure to work? Perhaps it would be better to recognize, as Carabillo of NOW put it, "Most women are only a husband away from welfare."[5] And it is likely that most two-parent families are only a job (and loss of health insurance) and a major illness away from poverty.

Churches and the Single Mother
Many churches haven't decided yet what to do about divorce and illegitimate children and tend to take the easiest way out. Unfortunately, it's relatively easy to let the white middle class divorced mother, or the white middle class pregnant teen who gets an abortion or puts her child up for adoption, continue in our midst, while we demonize the poor black single mother who was foolish enough to have sex and get pregnant before marriage, but had the good sense to not marry a drug addict.

Welfare is essentially available for women and children only and was started when the American society almost unanimously supported,

---

[4] Ibid., 491, italics by Sidel.
[5] Lewis D. Eigen and Jonathan P. Siegel, *The Macmillan Dictionary of Political Quotations*, (New York, NY: Macmillan, 1993), 704, quoted in R. Abelda, N. Folbre and the Center for Popular Economics, *The War on the Poor: A Defense Manual* (New York, NY: New Press, 1996), 105.

or even demanded, that a mother stay home to take care of her children. Many of the church leaders who vigorously attack the "lazy welfare queens" now, just a few years ago were preaching that mothers of their congregations with small children should stay home and take care of those children. The church needs to develop and apply a consistent theology and practice with the middle class and poor single mothers. This means having to deal with the growing need for two incomes to support a non-poor (middle class) lifestyle, the cost of childcare and welfare.

Gushee points out that this growing phenomenon of single mothers challenges the church to be different. To challenge the social norms that are encouraging single motherhood, Christians must first embody the "Christian sexual character within disciplined families and communities of faith."[6]

Jobs and All that Goes With'em

Jobs are the primary means of creating wealth for most Americans and are the focus of the problem among the poor, not only in this research, but in others. Respected author William Wilson said, "I was out in the field, looking at the notes and listening to the people, and it wasn't poverty that was coming up—it was jobs, jobs, jobs."[7]

The issues involved in jobs are multiple—reviving a work ethic among some poor, helping some to get and keep jobs, creating jobs that don't require extensive education and social skills, creating jobs that pay enough to live off of and providing the benefits necessary to health and productivity such as health care and child care.

Perhaps what this means for the church more that anything else is that the church is going to have to be involved in the community holisticly, for in a capitalistic society, it is in the market place and public forum that the conditions for jobs are created. Novak has accused the Roman Catholic Church of being anti-liberal society and anti-mercantile for some time now,[8] while Kristol sees the church in a

---

[6] David P. Gushee, "Rebuilding Marriage and the Family" in *Toward a Just and Caring Society,* ed. David P. Gushee (Grand Rapids, MI: Baker, 1999), 515.

[7] Christopher Shea, "William Julius Wilson Returns to the Debate on Poverty With a Book on the Impact of Jobs and Joblessness," *The Chronicle of Higher Education,* 4 October 1996, A12.

[8] Michael Novak, *The Spirit of Democratic Capitalism,* Touchstone ed. (New York: American Enterprise Institute and Simon and Schuster, 1983), 243-7.

"love-hate" relationship with Capitalism. "The act of commerce, the existence of a commercial society, has always been a problem for Christians."[9] He suggests that the reason is because the Christians lack the laws that Judaism and Islam have to "adapt to and live in an imperfect world."

Gay traces the development of Evangelical discussion of Capitalism, beginning with a scarcely a doubt of the religious validity of Capitalism, which was followed by such a strong defense that "McIntire all but equated modern industrial capitalism with the will of God in the world," to the neo-evangelical movement which lead to the rise of a "new" middle class, one made up of intellectuals.[10] This "new" middle class had its doubts about Capitalism, but it angered others and provoked a neo-fundamentalist movement that returned to a staunch defense of Capitalism. Schaeffer asks, "Is Capitalism Christian?" and concludes it is because "civil and religious freedom, progress and the preservation of human rights are inextricably linked with economic freedom," in other words, Capitalism.[11] Gonzalez's comparison of Jewish, Greek, Roman and early Christian economy, however, clearly demonstrates that modern day Capitalism is more deeply rooted in Roman economic practice than Christian economic practice.[12]

For too long, conservative Christians and churches have prooftexted the Bible to support Capitalism and ignored its influence on them. A medium sized church hires a married man with three children to work fulltime as a janitor and pays him $7 an hour, which comes to about $14,000 a year, which is the market price. This salary puts him well below the poverty line. Is this Christianity in action?

There are extensive new IRS regulations about the involvement of church in politics, but these do not prevent a Christian, or a church, from a non-partisan presence in the public debate. When the city council votes to give a tax break to a high tech firm that may move into the

---

[9] Irving Kristol, *Two Cheers for Capitalism* (New York: Basic Books, 1978), quoted in Warren T. Brookes, "Goodness and the GNP," (1985): 26-27, in *Is Capitalism Christian?* ed. Franky Schaeffer (Westchester, IL: Crossway Books, 1985).

[10] Craig M. Gay, *With Liberty and Justice for Whom?* (Grand Rapids: Eerdmans, 1991), 3, 10-18.

[11] Franky Schaeffer, *Is Capitalism Christian?* (Westchester, IL: Crossway Books, 1985), xvi-xvii.

[12] Justo L. Gonzalez, *Faith and Wealth: A History of Early Christian Ideas on the Origin, Significance and Use of Money* (San Francisco: Harper and Row, 1990), 28-68.

town and bring middle class workers with it, yet denies a tax break to a prospective retail mall that will employ hundreds of local residents at blue-collar wages, Christians need to be aware. It doesn't take a demonstration or political campaigning to inform voters.

Depression

While many of the needy, and wealthy, have clinical depression that needs professional help, probably most just need a friend to talk with. Perhaps the key is not counseling, but friendship, since a major problem mentioned above is the paternalism and trivialization that many of the poor suffer at the hands of good Christians. Nor do the poor need someone to solve their problems for them; they need companionship, someone to walk a difficult path with them. Goldstein emphasizes that case studies show that self-esteem is the primary factor in success of micro-enterprise training.[13]

Christians, as vessels of the great Counselor and as the uncircumcised adopted into God's family, ought to be the best of friends with the down and out, marginalized and vilified.

Putting It All Together

Chewning resisted the temptation to end his important four volume series on Biblical principles and public policy with a list of principles since he feared that they would become rules. He concludes

> It would be far better for all of us to continue a serious study of Scripture . . . The study of a list of principles, while undoubtedly increasing our knowledge, could well leave us with a conclusion that falls far short of the real lessons to be learned from this series.[14]

This author also emphasizes that the suggestions in the chapter are merely suggestion for starting the path to ministry with the poor. Reality will be more complex and difficult, but God will supply what is needed to accomplish his plans.

Chewning does, however, present a figure that expounds the overall principle presented in the series, seen in Figure 20.1. In this figure, public policy begins and ends with God who gave the standards for

---

[13] Donna M. Goldstein, "Microenterprise Training, Neoliberal Common Sense, and Self-Esteem," in *The New Poverty Studies,* ed. Judith Goode and Jeff Maskovsky (New York: New York University Press, 2001), 266.

[14] Chewning, "Biblically Authenticated Business," 300.

evaluating human endeavors, and their purpose is to glorify him. God provided some structures and work for humans in families, work and worship, and instructions on how they are to be done: righteousness-justice, loving kindness and humility. The desired human outcomes are the development of moral capital, human capital, and goods and services.

Chewning's figure is a strong reminder that the real purpose of ministry with the poor is not just changing the poor, but the transformation of all into Christ's likeness to God's glory.

Figure 20.1

Chewning's Biblically Authenticated Business, Economics, and Public Policy

(1) Standards for Evaluating Human Character and Conduct	(2) Human Activity Mandated by God	(3) Dimensions of Authenticated Work	(4) South-After Outcomes	(5) The Chief End
	Family	**Doing Justice-Righteousness (Relationally and as Stewardship: People and Resources)** a) Individual to Individual b) Individual to Institution and Community c) Institution and Community to Individual d) Institution and Community to Institution and Community e) Individual to Created Order	Development of Moral Capital	
Holy: Character of Attributes, Motives, Thoughts and Intentions		f) Institution and Community to Created Order		
God	Work	**Loving Mercy-Kindness** a) Charity toward "Neighbors" b) Concern for the Rights of the Powerless c) Distribution without Profits	Development of Human Capital	Glorify God
Righteous: Conduct Toward All Creation	Worship	**Walking Humbly with God** a) The Spirit with Which We Work b) Obeying When It is Uneconomical c) Enjoined / Empowered by God: Our Dependence	Development of Goods, Services, and Productive Capital	

CHAPTER 21
SUGGESTIONS FOR CHRISTIAN ACTION

Unfortunately, Western theology tends to be more ontological than practical.[1] Knowledge is not a virtue, nor is knowledge of evil the same as the desire to uproot it. True Biblical teaching does not lead to pious slogans, but to practice, since God himself is known more by his actions than his laws.

> God, according to the Bible, is known by what he does, . . . The covenant at Sinai, then, is not just a pious experience of God; it is a celebration of the God of liberation whose will is revealed in the freedom of slaves.[2]

Thus, interpretation of the Biblical text is not complete when Christians have thought about it, or even when they've taught it, but when they've lived it.

The purpose of this section is to provide some concrete steps and models for Christians and churches of varying abilities and resources to use as beginning points. These suggestions are not comprehensive strategies for defeating poverty; they are suggestions and examples of how other Christians and churches have made difference in their communities for the poor. The suggestions are not rules, but examples and injunctions to righteousness. Being just implies a quality of relationships and actions that have a rightness about them. The need to discuss

---

[1] Harvie M. Conn, "The Missionary Task of Theology: A Love/Hate Relationship?" *Westminster Theological Journal* 45 (Spring 1983): 14.
[2] James H. Cone, "Black Theology of Revolution, Violence and Reconciliation," *Union Seminary Quarterly Review* 31 (Fall 1976): 8-9.

rightness can be very frustrating; so many people look for rules by which to determine right from wrong.

> The desire for rules that somehow allow people to be righteous is a misguided but persistent longing in many hearts. A rule can commend righteousness but cannot embody it. . . . I become tense when righteousness is confused with rule keeping.[3]

Olasky points out that poverty is a complex situation and those who deal with it must "go dot to dot and draw a picture," not try to isolate and solve problems one at a time.[4] For that reason, the strategies below are not developed as specific answers to the four issues above. Each of those issues is holistic, and each individual issue may need several of the suggestions below for improved conditions. This section begins with guiding principles and specific suggestions in the areas of personal relationships and follows with suggestions about the secondary relationships of economics, social interaction and politics.

Guiding Principles

The suggestions below are based on three fundamental principles of action. First, God only expects each one to do what he can do, not more, nor less. Too often, Christians and churches avoid getting involved because the problem is so large and they can't see how they can solve everyone's problem. Well, neither of those is expected. God will provide what is necessary to achieve his goals, and as the second principle says, most of the poor want to solve their own problems; they just need some help. The third principle is to be very careful with government involvement. This doesn't mean to avoid having any influence or connection with the political powers, but it does mean that government programs for the poor are entitlements, or rights, based on the libertarian nature of American politics.[5] This "I've got a right to receive your help" and federal regulations can be more of a burden than a help. Besides, as Henry puts it, "justice is the course that neighbor love

---

[3] Richard C. Chewning, "Biblically Authenticated Business, Economics, and Public Policy," in ed. Richard C. Chewning, *Biblical Principles and Public Policy: the Practice*, Christians in the Marketplace Series (Colorado Springs: Navpress, 1991), 299.

[4] Marvin Olasky, *Renewing American Compassion* (New York: Free Press, 1996), 187.

[5] Lawrence M. Mead, *Beyond Entitlement* (New York: Free Press, 1986), 1.

takes."[6] Justice is more often a person's way of acting than an institution's way of acting.[7]

Developing Relationships with the Poor

As demonstrated in the discussion of Nehemiah, the single most important thing a Christians can do to help the poor is go beyond barriers and stereotypes to being with the poor, to developing a personal relation with a poor person, preferably one that challenges the Christian. This is a constant theme among proven Christian organizations.

Barriers

The barriers people will face as they begin to step out of their routine and meet people who are different from they are illustrated in the discussion of Nehemiah above: a faulty vision of reality, fear, greed, egocentrism, fear of politics and lack of a long term commitment. Mason warns, however, in his reflection on Biblical public welfare, "when poverty afflicted some of the members of society, all members were to bear responsibility" and all were to respond.[8]

Outcomes Desired

The primary purpose is not so that all of one's middle class goodness and wisdom can rub off on others, but that both can grow. Both the Bible and experience speak to people in all circumstances, and Christians often miss wonderful lessons because they isolate themselves—"true development benefits us as much as it does the people."[9]

One way is to think of this relationship building as family building. When Mason considered how to apply Biblical principles to today's poverty situation, he called for the

---

[6] Carl F. H. Henry, "Linking the Bible to Public Policy," in *Biblical Principles and Public Policy: The Practice*, ed. Richard C. Chewning, Christians in the Marketplace Series (Colorado Springs: Navpress, 1991), 26.

[7] Reinhold Neibuhr, *Moral Man and Immoral Society* (New York: Charles Scribner's Sons, 1932, reprint 1960), 48.

[8] John D. Mason, "Biblical Principles Applied to a Public Welfare Policy," in *Biblical Principles and Public Policy: the Practice*, ed. Richard C. Chewning, Christians in the Marketplace Series (Colorado Springs: Navpress, 1991), 89.

[9] Paul G. Hiebert, "Anthropological Insights for Whole Ministries" in *Christian Relief and Development,* ed. Edgar J. Ellison (Dallas, TX: Word), 81.

restoring of the strong nuclear (if not extended) family. Where nat-
ural families do not exist, loose or tight surrogate families can be
found.[10]

Another way involves the church. This may require "re-evan-
geliz[ing] the church."[11] Churches that are more ontological than practical, disconnected from their community, who treat other people as
categories rather than individuals created by God and at the same reject
community in favor of extreme individualism for themselves, need to
be reacquainted with the good news of the Kingdom of God.[12]

How To Do It
Some may have an experience similar to the author who one day
inadvertently sat at "the blacks' table" in the school cafeteria. The re-
ception may have been cool. Where does someone meet people different from himself?
1. Many of our churches have poorer people in them, usually on
the fringe. Invite them for dinner.
2. Poor people are often not passive people waiting for someone to
come save them. If someone wants to get involved with poor people,
read the paper looking for where and when they are already meeting.
Then join in their project, accept their agenda as a starting place.
3. Volunteer at a Habitat for Humanity, Boys and Girls club,
senior citizens meal program, as a teacher's helper in the public
schools, local jails, community programs through the judicial system
such as CASA (a children's advocate group), local missions, thrift
stores.
4. Visit minority churches.
5. Find someone who can be an advocate for you in these groups.
6. Don't expect to be accepted heartily the first time one visits. If
one has an advocate, it will probably take at least six months to begin
to earn their trust, and without one, it may take several years.

To change anyone's worldview, the minister must earn the right to be
heard. This credibility develops through commitment and a
consistent presence in the community for several years. The urban

---

[10] Ibid., 92-93.
[11] J. N. J. Kritzinger, "Liberating Mission in South Africa" *Missionalia* 18 #1
(1990): 45.
[12] Mark 1:14-15.

church planter will often need to force himself or herself into a wider area of daily life in the city as a continual learner.[13]

7. Of course, socio-cultural adjustments will have to be made. For example, Caucasians in predominately black areas may avoid eye contact in order to avoid presenting a possibly challenging look. But in southeastern Louisiana, African American men acknowledge one another through a nod, greeting or wave when they pass on the street. Imitating that custom seems to be the best choice for Caucasian men.

8. It is so important that it bears repeating: whatever group one may find to enter, one will have to accept their agenda to begin work. That is the purpose of this research project, to identify how some poor people are thinking about the causes of poverty.

Building Community Among the Poor

In contrast to the individualistic methods commonly proposed to help the poor, community is most likely the answer. Berger insists that community, a cognitive minority, is necessary in order to maintain a less ideologized worldview.[14] It is only in "Abrahamic minorities," as Camara called them,[15] that the church can break down the extreme individualism and dichotomization of reality common to "White Christianity" and build a holistic functioning of Christianity.[16]

The goal of community development is empowerment through the cooperation of poor people with each other. Despite the overuse of "empowerment" that has turned many conservative Christians away from it, Mason asserts that the Bible does speak of the rights of the

---

[13] Evertt W. Huffard, "Principles from *Urban Mission*, 1983-1992," paper read at 1993 Urban Ministries Conference, Houston, TX (1993): 1, referencing Rick Tobias and Larry Matthews, "Evergreen-Ministry Shaped by Need," *Urban Mission* #4 (1992): 38.

[14] Peter L. Berger, *A Rumor of Angels* Anchor Books ed. (New York: Doubleday, 1990), 19.

[15] Hélder Câmara, "Un pacto digno de coronar vuestra marcha" [A covenant worthy to crown your march], message to the youth movement *Mani Tese* [Out-stretched hands] climaxing a march on 5 November 1972, Plaza Michelangelo, Florence, Italy; in *Hélder Câmara: Proclamas a la Juventud* [Hélder Câmara: Proclamations to Youth], edited by Benedicto Tapia de Renedo, first volume of a trilogy, with introduction by editor, Serie PEDAL 64 (Salamanca: Ediciones Sígueme, 1976), 189.

[16] Kritzinger, "Liberating," 47.

poor.[17] This is not the right to be lazy and supported by others, but the right to justice.

Linthicum's book, *Empowering the Poor* (1991), is an excellent handbook on how to build community that will empower the poor, but Maduro clarifies that this "prophetic movement" will be effective according to its group consciousness, organization and mobilization.[18] Gastil's *Democracy in Small Groups* (1993) and Slessarev's "Organizing the Poor" (1999) are also useful resources.[19] Shabecoff's *Rebuilding Our Communities* listed resource books and organizations in its appendices.[20] World Bank research has a useful comprehensive agenda for change and numerous case studies that measure effectiveness of different tactics.[21]

Some Christian organizations have been very successful in community development with spiritual methods and goals. They include The Christian Community Development Association, World Vision and MARC (its publishing organization), Urban Mission magazine and the Mennonite Central Committee.

Helping People Have Decent Income through Jobs
In today's modern capitalistic economy, jobs are the key for most people to support themselves. This section includes not only suggestions on how to help poor people find and keep jobs and how churches can influence wages, but also about how churches can help create jobs or encourage low income adults to become entrepreneurs.

---

[17] Mason, "Biblical Principles," 88.

[18] Otto Maduro, *Religion and Social Conflicts,* trans. by Robert R. Barr, (Maryknoll, NY: Orbis, 1982), 136-9.

[19] John Gastil, *Democracy in Small Groups* (Philadelphia: New Society Publishers, 1993) and Helene Slessarev, "Organizing the Poor" in *Toward a Just and Caring Society,* ed. David P. Gushee (Grand Rapids, MI: Baker, 1999), 396-426.

[20] Alice Shabecoff, *Rebuilding Our Communities* (Monrovia, CA: World Vision, 1992), 267-79.

[21] Deepa Narayan, Robert Chambers, Meera Kaul Shah, and Patti Petesh, *Crying Out for Change* Voices of the Poor Series (New York: Oxford University Press, 2000): 266-89 and Deepa Narayan and Patti Petesch, *From Many Lands* Voices of the Poor Series (New York: Oxford University Press, 2002).

Finding and Keeping jobs

Guglar pointed out that "access [to jobs] is largely a function of three criteria: education and training, gender, and patronage"[22]—especially patronage. He clarified why—"Many employers . . . know that skills and knowledge are not as important for many positions as other qualities: dependability, potential for training, persistence, and initiative.[23] Both the literature review and the interviews revealed the importance of finding jobs through a network of family and friends. Thus, the first task to help poor people find jobs, or better jobs, is to get to know the poor people.

The second task may be, depending on the individual, training the person to how to work, how to interview for jobs and "life management skills."[24] Davis recommends mentoring for young black men of the inner city.[25] He suggests exposing them to successful black men and teaching self-discipline through Christian mentoring to prepare them for work. Goldstein clarifies that even in micro enterprise training, the key factor influences success is self-esteem.[26]

There are numerous life skills courses that Christian organizations use, besides the numerous government programs that teach work skills, interviewing skills and building resumes. The US military also has had decades of training people with low education for highly skilled jobs.

The most important task, however, is acting as a "broker" for the unemployed person.[27] This normally includes helping the person find a job, arrange reliable transportation and keep the job. For those who have never had a formal job before, a low paying or free internship may be the first step.

---

[22] Josef Gugler, "Introduction," in *The Urbanization of the Third World*, ed. Josef Gugler (New York: Oxford University Press, 1988), 55.

[23] Ibid., 56.

[24] Richard C. Chewning, "Editor's Perspective" in *Biblical Principles and Public Policy: the Practice*, ed. Richard C. Chewning, Christians in the Marketplace Series (Colorado Springs: Navpress, 1991), 98.

[25] Harold Davis, *Talks My Father Never Had with Me* (Champaign, IL: KJAC Publishing, 1995), 5.

[26] Donna M. Goldstein, "Microenterprise Training, Neoliberal Common Sense, and Self-Esteem," in *The New Poverty Studies,* ed. Judith Goode and Jeff Maskovsky (New York: New York University Press, 2001), 266.

[27] Tony L. Whitehead, "The Buccra-Massa and the Little Man's Broker in a Jamaican Sugartown" *Social Science and Medicine* 19 #5 (1984): 561-72.

Chewning also points out a useful political goal related to finding jobs: the passage of a meaningful tax incentive for businesses "to find, train, and employ people living in poverty."[28]

Creating jobs and Influencing Wages

City governments will discourage or encourage the locating or development of potential large-scale employers because of the type of jobs they will offer. According to one report, the city of San Antonio spurned the construction of a large automobile plant because they were worried it would raise wages!

> Like the pecan trees that shade the Alamo, low wages have fig-ured prominently in San Antonio's economic landscape as long as anyone can remember. When an automobile manufacturer tried to open a plant there in the 1930s, local business leaders spurned it, worried that a large union shop would drive up wages citywide. Four decades later, in a report aimed at luring new businesses to the area, the city's Economic Development Foundation continued to promote San Antonio as a haven of cheap labor.[29]

The Industrial Areas Foundation is nation wide alliance of commu-nity organizations that "share a vision in which all citizens can take part in shaping the political decisions that affect their lives."[30] "IAF affiliates . . . stress building relations with business leaders, public officials, and other traditional power brokers."[31]

As mentioned earlier, new businesses can be started for the purpose of employing welfare or homeless people. The Mennonite Central Committee has successful work programs in construction and landscaping in Edmonton.[32] Food and Hunger Hotline in New York is another example.[33] The great Voice of Calvary ministry in Jackson,

---

[28] Chewning, "Editor's Perspective," 97.

[29] Christopher Reardon, "A Living Wage," *Ford Foundation REPORT*, Sum-mer-Fall 1995, 8.

[30] Ibid.

[31] Ibid., 9.

[32] Bruce W. Wilkinson, "Biblical Principles and Unemployment," in *Biblical Principles and Public Policy: the Practice*, ed. Richard C. Chewning, Chris-tians in the Marketplace Series (Colorado Springs: Navpress, 1991), 73.

[33] Michael Ryan, "This restaurant serves up opportunity—and the food's good too!" *Parade Magazine*, 24 December 1995, 8.

Mississippi found unused farmland, raised produce and sold it at their thrift store to poor city dwellers.[34]

Entrepreneurship

Grigg outlines possible means of helping the poor for the wealthy and middle class Christians. What he recommends for the wealthy Christian is to aid through capital investment in vocational training, cooperatives, small businesses, housing and tools.[35] Wilkinson pointed out the Bible "emphasizes the ownership and working of one's own property rather than the increasing concentration of wealth and more wage or salary level."[36] The World Bank reports that poor people throughout the world regard self-employment as the most reliable method of economic improvement.[37]

Grigg suggests that only 25% of the new business start-ups will be entirely successful and another 25% are partially successful,[38] but there are several examples of organizations providing startup capital for small businesses that have very good success rate. Opportunity Network has made 46,000 loans and created 78,000 jobs from 1981 to 1993.[39]

Very small service businesses may be attainable with very little capital. Bromley classifies several useful types of occupations that are common in urban centers: retail distribution, small-scale transport, personal services such as shoe shining and typing, and recycling.[40] Some of these probably require licenses. While these may be beginning points, they are precarious.[41]

Shipp criticized the individualistic nature of most economic community development models. Reviewing models of economic development by the Mondragon Cooperative Movement, Booker T. Washington, the American government's Economic Community Development Corporation, Marcus Garvey and W. E. B. Du Bois, Shipp identified

---

[34] Tom Sine, *The Mustard Seed Conspiracy* (Waco, TX: Word, 1981), 192-193.

[35] Viv Grigg, *Cry of the Urban Poor* (Monrovia, CA: MARC, 1992), 277.

[36] Wilkinson, "Biblical Principles," 63, 66.

[37] Narayan et al, *Crying,* 65-8.

[38] Grigg, *Urban Poor,* 268.

[39] Ronald J. Sider, *Genuine Christianity* (Grand Rapids: Zondervan, 1996), 145.

[40] Ray Bromley, "Working in the Streets: Survival Strategy, Necessity, or Unavoidable Evil?" in *The Urbanization of the Third World,* ed. Josef Gugler (New York: Oxford University Press, 1988), 161-162.

[41] Ibid., 167.

the Modragon model as the only one that really worked. It is "reputedly
the most significant cooperative system in the industrialized world."[42]
The other models reviewed did cause some new minority owned businesses to open, but very few jobs resulted.[43] According to Morrison,
begun in the 1950's in the Basque region of Spain, the Mondragon
system created 170 co-ops, providing "21,000 well paying jobs."[44] The
key characteristics were

> (1) it serves an oppressed ethnic minority; (2) its primary objective is
> collective economic advancement; (3) it avoids control by a technical
> or managerial elite; (4) it promotes democratic control of its gov-
> erning structures; (5) it makes social development an essential goal
> of economic development; (6) it requires cooperative entrepre-
> neurship; (7) it provides comprehensive social services and training;
> and (8) its economic activities expand beyond the ethnic group and
> local market.[45]

Shipp's greatest emphasis, however, is cooperative entrepreneurship, not individualistic entrepreneurship. Individual entrepreneurship
seemed to inevitably lead to "profit-making ethos" and only individual
gain.[46]

Conditions that Encourage Productivity

Grigg outlines two ways wealthier churches can be effective working with the poor. One way mentioned is through the money, the
capital for start up of small businesses and service organizations such
as nurseries. "Far more important is giving personnel who can impart
spiritual life and technical skills."[47] There are certain conditions that
form the base or instruments for individuals to succeed. These include
useful education, health care availability, childcare availability, transportation, housing and safety.

---

[42] Sigmund C. Shipp, "The Road Not Taken: Alternative Strategies for Black
Economic Development in the United States," *Journal of Economic Issues* 30
(March 1996): 80.

[43] Ibid., 85.

[44] Roy Morrison, *We Build the Road As We Travel* (Philadelphia: New Society
Publishers, 1991), quoted in Shipp, "The Road Not Taken," 3, 8.

[45] Shipp, "The Road Not Taken," 82.

[46] Ibid., 85.

[47] Grigg, *Cry*, 275.

Education

Education is almost unanimously assumed in the United States, and by the informants, to be the primary means of alleviating poverty. This despite the fact that it has been basis of the unsuccessful War on Poverty for decades. The educational system in the U.S. has become incredibly powerful through its subtle teaching of values and presuppositions. Schlossberg says, "One of the most useful tools in the quest for power is the educational system"[48] because the power of assumption is so great. Assumptions, in fact, are more powerful than assertions, because they bypass the critical faculty and thereby create prejudice.[49]

The problem seems to have been the type of education that American public schools have been delivering. According to Freire, true education is learning to see, interpret and act on the reality in which one live.

> This then is why I say that "education as the practice of freedom" is not the transfer, or transmission of knowledge or cultures. Nor is it the extension of technical knowledge. It is not the act of depositing reports or facts in the educatee. It is not the "perpetuation of the values of a given cultural." It is not "an attempt to adapt the educatee to the milieu.". . . In the educational process for liberation, educator-educatee and educatee-educator are both cognitive Subjects before knowable objects which mediate them.[50]

Thus, while it is heartily recommended to volunteer at local public schools, assist in civic and business attempts to bolster the schools, etc., the matter deserves broader thought as well. Some serious questions need to be answered through civic and school organizations.

First, all agree that parents are a key for success in school. According to Skillen, low-income families are forced to use the (often poor) government schools because the alternatives are too costly. He recommends recognition that (1) parents are the principle responsible for the education of their children, not the state, (2) schools are entities

---

[48] Herbert Schlossberg, *Idols for Destruction: The Conflict of Christian Faith and American Culture* (Wheaton, IL: Crossway Books, 1990), 209.
[49] Ibid., 210.
[50] Paulo Freire, *Education for Critical Consciousness*, trans. and ed. by Myra Bergman Ramos (New York: Continuum, 1990), trans. from *Educação como Prática da Liberdade* (Rio de Janeiro: Editora Paz e Terra, 1969) and *Extención y Comunicación* (Santiago: Institute for Agricultural Reform, 1969), 149.

of themselves and are not merely extensions of the government or parents, and (3) parents should be given tax credits or vouchers to allow true choice in schooling, or better yet, all schools should be eligible for parental selection and public funding.[51] While the growing home school movement has demonstrated its success at teaching children,[52] social workers and school officials tend to suspect minority or low-income homeschoolers.[53]

Second, are schools teaching skills that are needed on jobs? Or more importantly, are schools teaching students how to learn so that they can continue to grow with the technology? With the push to meet standards on national tests there is the tendency to teach for the tests rather than teach for life. Americans also have an infatuation with college studies so that adequate vocational training is overlooked for the many people who never go to college.

Third, are schools emphasizing self-esteem and making allowances to the degree that students aren't learning? Glenn charges that many schools assume that minority children have low self-esteem and different cultures, and so schools must compensate for that by requiring less from them than they do from majority children.[54]

Fourth, are technical colleges accredited so that their graduates really can qualify for a job? Perhaps a local church or two can operate a free tutoring course for students and parents. Materials and suggestions are available at local school supply stores and home schooling resources.

True emphasis on education probably means better teachers. Some Christians already have taken teaching in difficult areas as their mission; may there be many more! On a political agenda, better teachers will probably be more likely with higher wages and less union control.

---

[51] James W. Skillen, "Biblical Principles Applied to a National Education Policy," in *Biblical Principles and Public Policy: the Practice*, ed. Richard C. Chewning, Christians in the Marketplace Series (Colorado Springs: Navpress, 1991), 226-227, 229.

[52] Home School Legal Defense Association, "Nationwide Study of Home Education," *Home School Court Report*, December 1990, 6; David Sharp, "Your Kids' Education is At Stake," *USA Weekend* 14-16 March 1997, 4.

[53] Home School Legal Defense Association. *Oklahoma: Unusual Activity in Oklahoma Courts,"* Home School Court Report 11 (December/January 1995/1996): 12.

[54] Charles L. Glenn, "Just Schools" in *Toward A Just and Caring Society,* ed. David P. Gushee (Grand Rapids, MI: Baker, 1999), 310-2.

Health care

Cochran says,

> [h]ealth care touches the heart of the gospel. . . . Even more pro-
> foundly, Jesus does not simply *heal* the sick; he *identifies himself*
> *with the sick.*[55]

It has probably concerned many that "[e]mployer-provided
medical insurance is slowly cracking,"[56] but for many lower income
people, it's already gone. Poor health and nutrition is major problem
for the poor despite Medicaid and other government health care. One
can begin to appreciate the problem by simply going with poor person
to health clinic. Scheduling, transportation and availability seem to be
the major problems for low-income families.

Free or government subsidized health care is frequently booked up
for weeks in advance, so the poor person usually has to go to a private
clinic and pay or wait until the problem is so severe that a visit to the
emergency room is necessary.

Transportation to and from the clinic can also be difficult to
families without cars, and poor families frequently have to pay
someone to take them. Also when a family member is in the hospital,
others may not be able to visit because of the lack of transportation. A
church could begin a transportation ministry for the poor.

The biggest problem is the lack of affordable medical care for the
working poor. The cost of medical care is escalating. In 1986, medical
expenditures were 11% of the U.S. Gross National Product and 50%
more than the "enormous" expense on national defense.[57] At that time,
annually half a million people had medical expenses greater than 50%
of their annual income, and 7 million people had expenses greater than
15% of the annual income.[58]

As mentioned earlier, a common reason for the return to welfare is
to obtain necessary medical care. While a national health care program

---

[55] Clarke E. Cochran, "Health Policy and the Poverty Trap" in *Toward A Just
and Caring Society,* ed. David P. Gushee (Grand Rapids, MI: Baker, 1999),
234.

[56] Mason, "Biblical Principles," 66.

[57] James W. Henderson, "Biblical Principles Applied to a National Health Care
Policy," in *Biblical Principles and Public Policy: the Practice,* ed. Richard C.
Chewning, Christians in the Marketplace Series (Colorado Springs: Navpress,
1991), 237-238.

[58] Ibid., 238.

may or may not be a good idea, something needs to be done for the approximately 25% of American children without medical care. Many churches could start a health clinic by arranging space at a community center and asking doctors to donate one day per month.[59] Pre-natal and pediatric care are especially important.

Life skills labs also have good material on health, hygiene and pre-natal care. One church also provided free health, hygiene and grooming products for poor people since food stamps can't be use for them.[60]

Childcare

Lack of affordable childcare is another major reason for women to stay on or return to welfare. And those who are working are often severely hampered financially by the cost they are paying. In the city where this research took place, the author knows of two businesses that offered to help two different churches to pay the start up costs and guarantee a minimum number of students for a several years to begin a pre-school program for their employees. Both were turned down. These churches could have accepted the offer and ministered to dozens of low income families through subsidized childcare with little cost!

Given the enormous experience churches have at teaching children and the investment in teaching facilities which are usually used only a few hours per week, churches ought to be leading the way to provide excellent, affordable child care, for the churches' benefit, if nothing else! One doesn't have to begin with a large facility, budget and organization. Christian women frequently take in a few children for extra income. Why not do it as a ministry instead of income?

Transportation

Transportation to get to work or medical care is another important barrier in which churches can make a difference. One strategy is to offer rides in conjunction with the services that may already be available for older people and through specialized service organizations.

Probably what would be an even more useful strategy is to help a poor person obtain the license and capital to run a bus route or begin to publicize the need for cheap transportation through the media and political connections.

---

[59] Gray Temple, Jr., *52 Ways to Help Homeless People* (Nashville, TN: Thomas Nelson, 1991), 135-6.
[60] MACS, 1930 Union Ave., Memphis, TN 38104, (901) 272-3700.

Housing

One of the keys to family success seems to be the security and ability for a family to promote a positive family lifestyle and culture. A decent and safe home is very important. There are numerous organizations making a difference in the housing for the poor. Shabecoff's *Rebuilding Our Communities* is an excellent resource of types of housing needed, examples of successful organizations and addresses. It also includes a discussion of creative loans for homeownership. Fanny Mae and Freddie Mac are useful sources of loans for home ownership that are available through local banks.

Temple suggests learning about the rent structure in the community and talking with local landlords to "tithe" their housing to provide low cost housing for a shelter.[61] And one can talk with developers about where service people for the expensive additions they're building are going to live.[62]

Habitat for Humanity is an international Christian organization that is building simple, decent houses all over the world. It is not a give away program, nor does it provide rental property. Habitat, through thousands of local affiliates in the United States and hundreds of international affiliates wants to give poor families not only a decent home, but also an opportunity to build equity. The homes are built by volunteers and the future homeowners, who have to work without pay about 500 hours to build "sweat equity." The homes are then sold to the poor family at cost and with no interest.

Transformation of the "ghettos" is also underway in some cities. HUD (Housing and Urban Development Agency) is transforming ghettos into safe stable neighborhoods through simple steps such as renovating the buildings so that each family has an outside entrance, owner occupied units, integrating commercial sites in the neighborhood and attracting "yuppies" to the area through innovative financing.[63]

Churches are also transforming their neighborhoods, such as the Evangelical Free Church of the Rock and Circle Urban Ministries in Chicago. The ministry identified the owners of the apartment buildings in their neighborhood, kept track of the property tax situation, broke into the secret incestuous relationship between the owners and tax officials and bought several units at the auctions of repossessed buildings.

---

[61] Temple, *52 Ways,* 127-8, 113-4.
[62] Ibid., 118-9.
[63] Blair Kamlin, "Housing That Works," *Chicago Tribune,* 18 June 1995, sec. 1 p. 1, 8-9; "Breaking Ground," *Urban Village* 11 #4 (December 2005): 3.

These buildings are then reformed and made safe. All the rent income is reinvested in upkeep of the building.[64] Another church has not had such success,[65] so expertise is required.

On the political agenda, Mason emphasized the destructive isolation and stigmatation of "projects" and recommended housing vouchers instead of housing projects.[66]

Safety

Safety is another condition that facilitates success. Unsafe neighborhoods contain many good solid citizens. The key to most community development projects is the unification of powerless individuals into a powerful group. "The poor can be empowered only by acting collectively through reflection, projects and actions."[67]

While there are federal grants available to local police forces to enact community policing which can be effective, eventually the police will leave and the responsibility will fall back on the community. A group of neighbors who form an association, meet regularly with police and politicians, attend town meetings, succeed in getting media coverage and network with other service organizations will more likely be attended more promptly than a "crank call" reporting another crime in progress in a high crime area. One example is the Queen City Congress in Charlotte where the poorer neighborhoods partnered with the nearby wealthier neighborhoods to fight together rather than against each other.[68]

Plesha, urban ministries coordinator of Colorado Christian University, suggests getting to know the police in the neighborhood; flag'em down if necessary.[69] A minister can volunteer as a chaplain for the police, and a church can host a dinner in their honor.[70]

---

[64] Raleigh Washington, presentation made to class on Relief and Development Ministries visiting from Trinity Evangelical Divinity School, Deerfield, IL, July 23, 1991).

[65] Alex Kotlowitz, "Being a Landlord is a Mixed Blessing for Chicago Church," *Wall Street Journal*, 2 April 1992, A1, A8, 1.

[66] Mason, "Biblical Principles," 86.

[67] Robert C. Lithicum, *Empowering the Poor* (Monrovia, CA: MARC, 1991), 38.

[68] Neal Peirce, "A New Day for Charlotte's Activist Neighborhoods," *New Orleans Times-Picayne*, 3 July 1995, B7.

[69] Jo Kadlecek, "Coping with Crime in the 'Hood," *Restorer* 6 (Fall 1995): 3.

[70] Temple, *52 Ways*, 72-5.

Political Influence

While it is strongly recommended that Christians develop relationships and influence the political structures of their communities, it is also strongly recommended that this be done with care. "Both the evangelical left and right, it seems, have become quite anxious about the power of the modern state." One sees it as power controlled by liberal bureaucrats; the other as power controlled by wealth.[71] But a Christian can't deny one's part in politics. Christians pay local, state and federal taxes to governments, and vote to choose policies and people to lead the government.

Issues for Political Involvement

The problem is that many Christians that are involved in politics appear to be trying to "gore another's ox," that is, strengthen themselves at the expense of another.[72] Skillen pointed out that

> entire issue of religion versus secularity . . . might have never become an issue if the nineteenth-century Protestants had not tried to remove Catholic schools from public recognition on the grounds that they were "parochial" and "sectarian."[73]

The purpose of political involvement for the Christian is the "good of the entire community."[74]

Political awareness and activism is necessary to help the poor because the federal and state governments control so much. Olasky gave numerous examples of how foolish regulations inhibit charities from accomplishing their work, such as requiring a wheelchair ramp for a shelter for prostitutes or an elevator in shelter run by nuns who had taken a vow of poverty. Fear of being sued prevents doctors from working at free clinics and keeps businessmen from hiring "risky" employees.[75] Bureaucrats often seem to be more interested in preserving their jobs than serving the needy.[76] Local officials attract or repel new businesses and consequently new jobs.

---

[71] Craig M. Gay, *With Liberty and Justice for Whom?* (Grand Rapids: Eerdmans, 1991), 94.

[72] Chewning, "Editor's Perspective," 232.

[73] Skillen, "National Education Policy," 227.

[74] Chewning, "Editor's Perspective," 232.

[75] Marvin Olasky, *Renewing American Compassion* (New York: Free Press, 1996), 101-105.

[76] Ibid., 12.

In the larger realm, the biggest area is the government decisions about tax structures, fiscal policy, trade and economics, civil rights, social welfare, etc. Olaski and others present a number of tax issues that could help alleviate poverty.[77] Sider discusses numerous structural problems that require political action for improvement.[78]

How to Get Involved

Phillips' *The Blue Book for Grassroots Politics* is a manual for political involvement on the local and state level regardless of one's political persuasion. His book is particularly useful because he explains the differences between non-profit organizations and political action committees and how each should be registered with the government and IRS.[79]

Phillips emphasizes four points to begin this work: know the rules by which the government works, know the players (politians and influential supporters), participate and organize.[80] One needs to gather information: read a civics book, read the paper for current issues and community meetings, attend some meetings just to meet people, visit city hall and ask for an organizational chart of how the local government opperates, etc. Find out who prepares budgets.[81] If one is really serious, he can read the Congressional Report.

Phillips suggests that a Christian or person adopt a congressman to pray for, write, call, feed information.[82] A Christian can have much more impact when the politician knows her before the issue becomes hot. Ultimately, the affect desired is to influence the worldview of the politician, for it is the worldview that is the basis for all decisions and laws, basis for judgement and inspiration to action.[83] This can be done by supplying the politician with stories for speeches.[84]

---

[77] Ibid., 187-195; Angelini et al in Ibid., 116.

[78] Ronald J. Sider, *Rich Christians in an Age of Hunger*, 2nd ed. (Downers Grove, IL: Inter-Varsity Press, 1984), 191-222.

[79] Charles R. Phillips, *The Blue Book for Grassroots Politics* (Nashville, TN: Thomas Nelson, 1990), 36-73.

[80] Ibid., 29-33.

[81] Temple, *52 Ways*, 76-83.

[82] Phillips, *Blue Book*, 48.

[83] Mark R. Amstutz, *Christian Ethics & U.S. Foreign Policy* (Grand Rapids: Academie Books [Zondervan]), 25-28; Richard Bauckham, *The Bible in Politics* (Louisville, KY: Westminster/John Knox, 1989), 30.

[84] Temple, *52 Ways*, 76-83.

Os Guinness critiques the four methods commonly used by Christians seeking political power and then warns Christians away from them: conspiracy theories, absolute depictions of good and evil, denial of free speech and defamation of character.[85] These kinds of tactics will eventually only hurt the church and the poor. Rather than those kind of tactics, in extreme cases, Yoder calls for "revolutionary subordination."[86]

> Subordination is significantly different from obedience. The conscientious objector who refuses to do what his government asks him to do, but still remains under the sovereignty of that government and accepts the penalties which it imposes, or the Christian who refuses to worship Caesar but still permits Caesar to put him to death, is being subordinate even though he is not obeying.[87]

Conclusion

A final word about action—I have often felt overwhelmed by the enormous world of needy people that cry out for help. Sometimes I've been paralyzed by that huge task, and I've seen others paralyzed for years because they felt that they had to save the world and knew they couldn't. I've been blessed to come upon the concept of "Missio Dei" —that is the "Mission of God." I'm not responsible to save the world; that's God's prerogative. I am simply responsible to do what I can with what God has given me. I've learned to do what I can and not what I can't. Freedom! Freedom, not as an excuse, but to serve!

---

[85] David Prior, *Jesus and Power* (Downers Grove, IL: Inter-Varsity Press, 1987), 50-51.

[86] John H. Yoder, *The Politics of Jesus* (Grand Rapids, MI: Eerdmans, 1972), 181.

[87] Ibid., 212.

AUTHOR'S BIOGRAPHICAL SKETCH

Michael Landon was born and raised in Oklahoma where he was privileged to grow up in a working class Christian family. He graduated from Oklahoma Christian University with a BA in Bible and a BS in Chemistry, Harding University Graduate School of Religion with an MA in Ministry and Trinity Evangelical Divinity School with a PhD in Intercultural Studies. He also did graduate work at Abilene Christian University and Faculdade de Teologia Nossa Senhora de Assuncão.

Mike and his wife were blessed to work as missionaries in Sao Paulo, Brazil for eight years, where their three children were born. Mike has been a minister at Churches of Christ in Louisiana, Kansas and Connecticut and taught full-time at Barclay College in Kansas, Southwestern Christian College in Terrell, TX, and the Center for Christian Education in Irving, TX.

This book is based on Mike's dissertation research on the causes of poverty begun among the working poor in Brazil and finished among the working poor of Louisiana.

INDEX

Aaronson, Stephanie: 48, 50
Abelda, R.: 161
African-American: 5, 11-13, 16, 40-41, 45, 53, 66, 72, 81, 83-84, 92, 113, 115, 120-122, 161, 170-171, 173
Alcoholism: 29-31, 57, 85-90, 131
Allen, C.: 153
Amado, Jorge: 34
Amstutz, Mark: 184
Anabaptist: 145

Bauckham, Richard: 184
Bassuk, E.: 51, 54
Bassuk, Shari: 49, 51, 54
Becker, Gary: 40, 44
Bell Curve: 40-41
Berger, Peter: 171
Berkof, Hendrik: 146
Bible: 3-4, 7, 98, **122-155**, 160-172
Bob's Story: **69-78**
Boff, Clodovis: 1, 34-36, 150-152
Boff, Leonardo: 1, 150, 153
Brazil: 1, 4, 24, 153
Bromley, Ray: 175
Brooks, Margaret: 48-51, 54
Brown, A.: 51
Brown, Robert: 140
Brueggemann, Walter: 153
Buckner, John: 48-51

Camara, Helder: 171
Cardoso, Fernando: 34, 37
Carla's Story: **69-73, 78-79**
Catholic Church: 1, 25-26, 99-100, 102, 104, 145, 162, 183
Chambers, Robert: 54, 172, 175
Cherry, Robert: 11, 12
Chewning, Richard: 134-135, 164-166, 168-169, 173-174, 179, 183
Chilcote, Ronaldo: 34
Childcare: 48-50, 78-79, 162, 176, 180
Children, Inappropriate Discipline: 44, 57, 100, 102, 107
Children, Early in Life: 14, 29-31,41-45, 75-79, 87, 95, 100, 102, 104

Churches: **75-77**, 87, **95-98**, 110, 112-115, 135-136, 139-142, **159-165**, 167-185, see also Catholic Church
Circle Urban Ministries, Chicago, Illinois: 181
Cochran, Clarke: 179
Cohen, L.: 127
Coleman, Richard: 30
Commons, John: 12
Community Development: 3, 169-172, 175
Cone, James: 167
Conn, Harvie: 167
Corcoran, Mary: 39-46, 59
Correlated Disadvantages: see Human Resources
Courts / Jail: 42-44, 92, 95, 100, 105, 137, 170
Culture of Poverty: 4-5, 9, **11-19**, 21, 39-46, 59-61, 86, 94-97, 117-122, 133
Culture vs. Structure Dichotomy: 39, 122

Davis, Harold: 173
Dawson, John: 142
Debt: 15, 31, 34-35, 78, 95, 100, 102, 108, 110, 131, 133
Demonization of Poor: 2, 50-51, 160-161
Dependency Theory: 9, 21, **33-38**, 150
Depression: see also Stress
Dietz, Gottfried: 125
Disability: 81, 91, 93, 95, 97
Discrimination: 75, 85-87, 97, 104-105, 115
Divorce: 90-91, 95, 97, 100-106, 107, 122, see also Single Mother
Don's Story: **81-87**
Durkheim: 38
Drugs: 71-73, 85-86 , 116

Early Church Fathers View of Wealth: 143-144
Economic Ethos Model: 4-5, 9, **21-28**, 29, 59-61, 106, 119-122
Edelstein, Joel: 34
Education: 14, 17, 22, 28, 31, 35, 41-43, 50, 69, 76-79, 83-87, 90-94, 99, 104-105, 108, 121, 162, 176-178
Eigen, Lewis: 161
Ely, Richard: 11-12
Entrepreneur: 175-176
Evelyn's Story: **89-98**
Exodus: 132-133

Fagan, Patrick: 40, 42
Family Needs: 48, 79, see also Childcare and Health Care
Family, Extended: 14, 17, 71-72, 75-76, 81, 93-94, 109-110, 113, 115-
    116, see also Culture of Poverty
Folbre, N: 161
Food and Hunger Hotline, New York: 174
Foster, Richard: 145
Friere, Paulo: 177

Gans, Herbert: 18
Gastil, John: 172
Gay, Craig: 130, 163, 183
Gettleman, Marvin: 16
Gilbert, Dennis: 33
Glenn, Charles: 178
God: 4, 6, 104-105, 136-137, see also Bible
Goertz, Hans-Jurgen: 142
Goldstein, Donna: 164, 173
Gonce, R. A.: 12
Gonzalez, Justo: 125-126, 143-144, 163
Goode, Judith: 39, 45, 47-48
Grigg, Viv: 132, 175-176
Gugler, Josef: 173
Guinness, Os: 185
Gushee, David: 162, 172, 178-179
Gutierrez, Gustavo: 26, 150

Habitat for Humanity: 170, 181
Hammond, Louisiana: 5, **65-67**, 69, 90
Hanks, Thomas: 132
Harrington, Michael: 16-17
Harris, Kathleen: 41
Harrison, Lawrence: 21-26
Hartman, Hiedi: 48, 50
Hauser, Stuart: 54
Haveman, R.: 40
Health Care: 17, 22, 28, 31, 35, 48-51, 101, 111, 162, 176, 179-180
Henderson, James: 179
Henry, Carl: 169
Hernstein, Richard: 40, 43
Herskovits, Melville: 12
Hess, Daniel: 35

Hiebert, Paul: 60, 154, 169
Hinkelammert, Franz: 34
Hispanics: 6, 11-13, 23, 66, see also Latin Ethos
Hofstede, Geert: 26
Homelessness: 56-58, 111-112, 174, 180
Home School Legal Defense: 178
Housing: 15, 17, 127, 176, 181-182
Huffard, Evertt: 171
Hughes, Richard: 153
Human Resources Model: 9, 39, **40-41**, 44, 119-122, 166

Ideology: 33, 36
Injustice / Oppression: 35-36, 83-87, 126-127, 131-133, 136-138, 150-
     152, see also Social Sin, Dependency Theory, U.S. Structural
     Model
Inner City: 45-46, see also Underclass Model
Intergenerational Poverty: see Culture of Poverty and U.S. Adaptations
     of Culture of Poverty

Jesus: 3-4, 131, 134, 139-141
Jobs: 15, 22, 31, 40-46, 48-49, 69, 73-79, 91, 94, 97, 100-101, 113,
     130, 134-136, 162-166, **172-176**, see also unemployment
Johnson, Lyndon: 13

Kadlecek, Jo: 182
Kahl, Joseph: 33
Kamlin, Blair: 181
Keefe, Thomas: 55
Kessler-Sklar, Susan: 48
Kleinman, Arthur: 53, 55
Koch-Schulte, Sarah: 28, 127
Kotlowitz, Alex: 182
Kowanick, Lucio: 34
Kozol, Jonathan: 57
Kristol, Irving: 163
Kritzinger, J.: 141, 170-171
Kuhn, Thomas: 154

Lamb, Richard: 56
Landon, Michael: 38, 138, 152
Latin Ethos: 23-27
Lausanne Committee for World Evangelism: 126-127

Leacock, Eleanor: 17-18
Lenin, Valdimir: 33
Lenz, Gabriel: 28
Lerner, Ralph: 24
Lernoux, Penny: 37, 65
Lewis, H.: 18
Lewis, Oscar: 11, **13-16**, 19
Liberation Theology: 4, 145, 148, 150-153, see Structural Sin Model
Lipset, Seymour: 28
Lithicum, Robert: 182
Lyon-Callo, Vincent: 56-57

MACS, Memphis, Tennessee: 180
Maduro, Otto: 172
Marmelstein, David: 16
Mary's Story: **99-106**
Marx, Karl: 12, 33, 38, 150-151, see also Dependency Theory
Maskovskey, Jeff: 39, 45, 47-48
Mason, John: 133-134, 169, 172, 179, 182
Material Resources Model: 9, 39, **43-45**, 59-61, 119-122
McCann, Dennis: 37
McClosky, Herbert: 29
McCloyd, V.: 53
McGrath, Marcos: 24
McLanahan: S.: 40
Mead, Lawrence: 42, 168
Media: 35, 75-77
Medieval View Of Wealth: 144-145
Micheo, Alberto: 34
Miguez-Bonino, Jose: 140
Miller, Walter: 18
Minimum Wage: 73-79, 113, 115
Missio Dei: 185
Moll, Peter: 37
Morrison, Roy: 176
Moser, Antonio: 61, 151-152
Mott, Stephen: 142, 146-148
Mouw, Richard: 146-148
Moynihan, Daniel: 16
Moynihan Report: 16
Muether, John: 144-145
Muntzer, Thomas: 142

Murrey, Charles: 40, 43, 45, 149
Myrdal, Gunner: 11-13

Narayan, Deepa: 28, 54, 127, 172, 175
National Security: 36
Nehemiah: 138, 169
Neibuhr, Reinhold: 169
Neo-conservatives: 148-150
Nida, Eugene: 27
North, Gary: 148-150
Novak, Michael: 23-27, 162-163

O'Brien, P.: 148
Olasky, Marvin: 168, 183-184
Olivia's Story: **107-117**
"Other America": 16-17

Parsons, Talcott: 59
Patel, Raj: 28, 127
Patron-Client Relationships: 35
Peirce, Neal: 182
Personal Irresponsibility: 2, 4-5, 9, 22, **29-31**, 43, 59-61, 85-86, 116,
    119-122, 136
Peterson, Randy: 145, 148
Petesh, Patti: 54, 172, 175
Philips, Charles: 184
Piotrkowski, Chaya: 48
Pixley, Jorge: 34
Political Action: 183-185
Poverty, Desperate: 1, 126-127
Prior, David: 185
Property: 15, 34-36, 125-126, 133, 137, 144
Prophets: 137-138
Protestant Work Ethic: 25
Psychological Problems: see Stress and Stress Model

Racism: 35, 41, 74-79, 83-87, 92, 94-97, 122
Rademacher, Anne: 28, 127
Rainwater, Lee: 30
Rangel, Carlos: 23-24
Rape: 53-54, 137
Reardon, Christopher: 174

Reformation View of Wealth: 144-145
Rich, Arthur: 35, 151-153
Roberts, Ron: 55
Rosenbaum, J.: 45
Ruth: 135-136
Ryan, Michael: 174

Sabbath: 129-131, 146
Safety: 127, 176, 182
Salomon, Amy: 47, 49, 51, 54
Sandefur, G.: 40
Schaeffer, Franky: 163
Schafft, Kai: 28, 127
Schlossberg, Herbert: 177
Schnitzer, Phoebe: 50, 53
Schwartz, Hans: 143
Shabecoff, Alice: 172
Shah, Meera: 54, 172, 175
Shea, Christopher: 45-46, 162
Shipler, David: 54
Shipp, Sigmund: 176
Sidel, Ruth: 2, 49, 130, 160-161
Sider, Ron: 145-146, 175, 184
Siegel, Jonathan: 161
Silence of Poor: 2-3
Simple Living Movement: 145-149
Sin: 131, 136, see also Social Sin
Sine, Tom: 175
Single Mothers: 14, 18, 40-43, 45-46, 50, 89, 91, 95, 97, 100-105, 113,
    135, 160-162
Skillen, James: 177, 183
Slessarev, Helene: 172
Slim, Hugo: 3
Smith, Adam: 24, 30
Snider, Noah: 130
Social Gospel: 12
Social Security: 85-86, 91
Social Sin: 35, see also Structural Sin
Southern, David: 12
Sorokin, Pitirim: 30
Sowell, Thomas: 29
Spain and its colonies: see Latin Ethos

Spalding, J.: 40
Stewart, Edward: 29
Stress: 9, 14, 17, 49, 54, 96, **99-102**, **108-116**, 127, 164
Stress Model: **53-57**, 59-61, 119-122
Structural Sin Model: 4-5, 21, 24, 59-61, 117, 138, 146, 151-152, see also Social Sin
Stott, John: 127, 153-154
Susser, Ida: 29

Talbot, John: 56
Tanaka, Yasumasa: 23
Taxes: 86, 135
Temple, Gray: 180-182, 184
Third World: 23-28, 34
Thiselton, Anthony: 153
Thompson, Paul: 3
Transportation: 48-50, 75-76, 176, 180
Trilateral Commission: 34

Uhlhorn, Gerhad: 143
Underclass Model: 9, 39, **45-46**, 59-61
Underdevelopment: see Economic Ethos
Unemployment: 18, 31, 48, 50
U. S. Structural Model: 9, **47-51**, 78-79, 86-87, 117

Valentine, Charles: 17-18
Voice of Calvary, Jackson, Mississippi: 174
Violence: 49, 51, 53-54, see also Safety and Stress

Wages, Low: 85-86, see also Minimum Wage
Walker, Amasa: 11
War on Poverty: 3, 16
Washington, Booker: 12, 174
Washington, Raleigh: 182
Weber, Max: 33, 38, 120, see Protestant Work Ethic
Weed, Michael: 153
Weinreb, L.: 51
Welfare: 1-2, 5, 41-43, 49-50, 73-73, 85, 90-91, 93-94, 98, 100-105, 110-116, 130, 160-162, 174, 179
Welfare Model: 9, 39, **42-43**, 45, 59-61, 76, 96, 119-122,
Whitehead, Tony: 173
"White Trash": 102